"The Saving" of America

"The "Saving" of America

Clifford Goldstein

Pacific Press Publishing Association
Boise, Idaho
Oshawa, Ontario, Canada

Edited by Lincoln E. Steed
Design by Tim Larson
Cover Illustration by Lynn Bernasconi
Type set in 10/12 Century Schoolbook

The author assumes full responsibility for all facts and quotations cited in this book.

ISBN 0-8163-0745-8

Library of Congress Catalog Card Number: 87-63360

88 89 90 91 92 • 5 4 3 2

Contents

Chapter 1

Marked Men

My first contact with Seventh-day Adventists was in 1979, in a little wooden health-food store in Gainesville, Florida. I didn't know they were Adventists. They didn't tell me, and it wouldn't have mattered if they had, because I knew nothing of their church. All I knew was that two days before I had given myself unconditionally, unreservedly, to Jesus Christ—and now I wanted to learn the Bible.

"What would you like to study?" asked Ronnie Fox, a short, energetic University of Florida student, who used the store as a campus outreach.

"I want to study prophecy," I answered. Then, as an afterthought (still not knowing they were Adventists), I added, "I want to study about America in prophecy. Is America in the Bible?"

For the next few days we met afterhours for Bible study. Among piles of this strange food (soy-bean hot dogs?) and, surrounded by walls papered with bright views of the Swiss Alps, we devoured the prophecies of Daniel 2 and 7. I was amazed to discover a description of the Roman church's role in endtime events. We progressed to Revelation 12 and 13, where that church was again described, this time in relationship to a new power, a lamblike beast with two horns who eventually speaks like a dragon. That new power, I saw, could only be the United States.

What made these prophecies so convincing was that while

we studied, John Paul II was on his first visit to the United States! An event unthinkable only a few years earlier, and yet so consistent with the prophetic outline.

The first time I ever read those prophecies concerning the United States and the papacy was as the pope paraded around the nation like a war hero. I learned about the predictions of future cooperation between the Vatican and Protestant America during the week *Time* magazine featured a picture of John Paul shaking hands with President Jimmy Carter on the White House lawn. The first time I ever heard of a coming unity between Protestants and Catholics was when the pope of Rome sang Wesleyan hymns with American Protestant leaders!

As the truth pierced my soul with power, I sat under those paper Alps and wept.

I soon became an Adventist too.

Four years later, November 1983, at Long Island, New York, I was researching an article about Martin Luther that I was writing for an Adventist magazine. I read these words that Luther had written during his last decade: "It is enough," he said. "I have worked myself to death. . . . I'll go lie down in the sand and sleep now. It is over for me, except for just an occasional little thwack at the pope."

Little thwacks? His most outrageous and filthy attacks were yet to come. I had been appalled, even offended, by Luther's scalding words for the pope, whom he called (among much worse things) "the bishop of sodomists" and "the scum of all the scoundrels in Rome."

No wonder all the bitterness between Catholics and Protestants for centuries.

Then, just after reading Luther's diatribes against the papacy, I picked up a *New York Times* for November 6, 1983, and read a headline: POPE PRAISES LUTHER ON PROTEST ANNIVERSARY.

My palms sweat on the newsprint.

It is January 1986. The Christian World Affairs Conference is held in Washington, D.C., sponsored by a New Right organization called FaithAmerica. Hundreds of conservative Christian preachers, educators, and leaders—a spectrum of American fundamentalism—came to discuss Strategic Defense Initiative, Sandinistas, the economy, AIDS, abortion, the Soviets, and tax reform. The speakers included presidential aspirant Jack Kemp, Secretary of Education William Bennett, Secretary of the Army John Marsh, and others.

I sat at a table and listened. Though in agreement with many of their positions, I didn't like the overt hostility to the separation of church and state. More than once, when someone attacked it, Amens! bellowed from the audience. Former Congressman John Conlan's statement that the phrase "separation of church and state" doesn't even appear in the American Constitution was instantly punctuated by Amens! from the faithful in the crowd. A true believer sitting on my right, a principal at a Christian school in New England, leaned over and with a big smile informed me that separation of church and state is found "in the Russian Constitution, not ours."

My heart pounding so hard it hurt, I went to the microphone in the audience and confronted not only the speaker of the moment, Congressman William Dannemeyer (R–California), but the entire group. The congressman had been talking about the need to bring "Judeo-Christian" values back to America. I asked him whether when he said Judeo-Christian, didn't he really mean Christian, and when he said Christian, didn't he really mean Protestant, and when he said Protestant, didn't he really mean fundamentalist? I then challenged the entire meeting about their hostility toward the separation of church and state, and I warned of the dangers in that which they advocated. While I was still standing, another congressman, Patrick Swindall (R–Georgia), attacked me from the podium. "You represent," he snapped, "the kind of person who doesn't know what the history of this nation is all about."

The audience exploded into clapping; others snickered in my face and—judging by the dirty looks—I saw how easily the lamb could speak as a dragon. Indeed, I had just tasted a bit of its fire.

Constitution Hall, September 17, 1986: Reverend Pat Robertson announced to the world that if within one year, "three million registered voters have signed petitions telling me that they will pray—that they will work—that they will give toward my election, then I will run as candidate for the nomination of the Republican Party for the office of the President of the United States of America."

The crowd erupted, as thousands stood, cheered, clapped, waved their arms in the air. The energy was fierce.

I sat in the press box, just in front of the stage. Peter Carlson from the *Washington Post* was at my right. Laurence Barrett from *Time* sat behind me. Journalists from all across America, even from Holland, Japan, Germany, and other nations filled the rows. Photographers had dragged in tons of camera and video equipment.

As I sat amid the lights, the noise, the music, I knew that prophetic history was being made. It didn't matter what happened to Robertson's campaign. Even if it flopped and he went back to faith healing, the fact that someone like him could be taken this seriously as a presidential candidate proved that America had reached a turning point in prophecy. Ten, fifteen years ago, Robertson would have been classified with all the scores of left- or right-wing extremists who every four years wage these ridiculous campaigns for the Oval Office. Yet, that night, Constitution Hall sizzled. Thousands of voters screamed, rows of international journalists scribbled on their pads, cameras clicked, and videos spun madly.

And though I wasn't waving my arms in the air or screaming, I was probably the most excited person there.

Or at least the second most excited there!

In front of me was Roland Hegstad, editor of *Liberty*

magazine, and for thirty years Adventism's leading defender of religious freedom. Because I had written numerous articles in his magazine against the type of church-state politics that Robertson espouses, and because I believe that Robertson represents those who will eventually take control of America, I felt scared, vulnerable that night because of what I had in print. As I watched what was happening around me, I suddenly knew that I was going to meet those articles again. And as I asked myself—*Did Roland see it this way, is it really that bad, am I just reading more into what was happening than was really there?*—he turned around, looked me in the face, and said, "We're marked men."

Chapter 2

People of the Prophets' Dreams

Imagine—the prophets. Daniel, Amos, Isaiah, Zephaniah, John—any of them, in dreams, in visions, taken into the secret counsels of God. Shown, perhaps, things that even angels hadn't seen. And often what they saw was the great day of the Lord and those who are living when it comes.

"Prepare to meet thy God, O Israel." Amos 4:12. "Seek ye the Lord, all ye meek of the earth, which have wrought his judgment; seek righteousness, seek meekness: it may be ye shall be hid in the day of the Lord's anger." Zephaniah 2:3. "The dragon was wroth with the woman, and went to make war with the remnant of her seed." Revelation 12:17.

Yet what the prophets saw only in vision, we see in person; what they had in symbols, we have in reality. Ours are the days the prophets dreamed about. Indeed, *we* are the people of their dreams.

Where are we in the tunnel of prophetic time? Where among the tens of thousands of verses in the Bible do we fit today? In Revelation 13, we see a beast coming out of the sea, a beast "having seven heads and ten horns" (verse 1), a blasphemous beast, a persecuting beast, a beast that had a deadly wound. Following that beast comes another, this time from out of the earth, a beast that has two horns like a lamb, yet speaks as a dragon. For years Adventists have identified this second beast as the United States. "I beheld another beast

13

coming up out of the earth; and he had two horns like a lamb, and he spake as a dragon." Verse 11.

Look carefully at this part of the text: "And he had two horns like a lamb, and he spake as a dragon."

Where are we in the Bible? We're at the comma between those two clauses. "And he had two horns like a lamb (*comma*) and he spake as a dragon." We sit at the comma today!

As Adventists, we have been blessed above all the nations of the earth. The words of Isaiah 5 are as much for us as they were for Judah: "Judge, please, between Me and My vineyard. What more could have been done to My vineyard that I have not done in it?" Verses 3, 4, NKJV. And we have been especially blessed in our understanding of last-day events.

While our brothers and sisters in other churches look to the Middle East—to wars in Palestine, to Jews in Israel, to a new temple in Jerusalem—we look at the churches themselves, to the pews and pulpits of Christendom, for we know that the churches *are* last-day events. While millions of Christians scan their Middle East maps about the impending "great controversy" between Russia and the Jews—the Battle of Armageddon—the real preparations for Armageddon are happening behind the stained-glass windows of their own sanctuaries. And while they speculate about the identity of the seven-headed beast of Revelation 13, we daily watch its growth, its progression, its healing.

Adventists associate themselves with the three angels of Revelation 14. We say we are the messengers symbolized by those angels, and we proclaim their messages to "every nation, and kindred, and tongue, and people." Revelation 14:6. We preach the "everlasting gospel," the news of a crucified and risen Saviour, Jesus Christ, who died for the sins of humanity. We proclaim that the "hour of his judgment is come" (verse 7), the time of the great preadvent judgment just prior to the second coming, when Jesus will return in the clouds and His reward shall be with Him. We herald the decree that "Babylon is fallen, is fallen" (verse 8), a warning against end-time religious and spiritual apostasy. And we give the final cry about the mark of the beast: "If any man worship the beast and his image, and receive his mark in his forehead, or in his hand, the same shall drink of the wine of the wrath of God" (verses 9, 10): a warning against false worship.

Intricately linked with these messages, particularly the third angel's message, is religious liberty. Though behind the scenes, the real issues deal with the character of God, the fairness of His law, and the great controversy between Christ and Satan, God's remnant people will face a more immediate struggle: the right to obey God's commandments though all the world be against them. According to the Bible, there will be no religious liberty for this tiny remnant, "an afflicted and poor people" (Zephaniah 3:12) who worship the Creator while the vast billions of the world "worship the beast and his image" (Revelation 14:9).

In *The Great Controversy* Ellen White writes that "as the Sabbath has become the special point of controversy throughout Christendom, and religious and secular authorities have combined to enforce the observance of the Sunday, the persistent refusal of a small minority to yield to the popular demand will make them objects of universal execration. It will be urged that the few who stand in opposition to an institution of the church and a law of the state ought not to be tolerated; that it is better for them to suffer than for whole nations to be thrown into confusion and lawlessness. . . . This argument will appear conclusive; and a decree will finally be issued against those who hallow the Sabbath of the fourth commandment, denouncing them as deserving the severest punishment and giving the people liberty, after a certain time, to put them to death."—Pages 615, 616.

Warning of the same event, the Bible says, "He had power to give life unto the image of the beast, that the image of the beast should both speak, and cause that as many as would not worship the image of the beast should be killed." Revelation 13:15.

Religious liberty, then, is part of the last warning message. We can't teach, preach, or even understand the third angel's message or last-day events without understanding the principles of religious freedom, because the most dramatic last-day events center on religious liberty.

Yet as a people, Seventh-day Adventists seem confused about religious liberty. Though we all know about the mark of the beast, impending Sunday laws, persecution and death decrees, many don't understand fully the principles of religious freedom, principles that can give us strength and encouragement for the coming crisis. Understanding the principles of religious liberty can help assure us that our positions are in harmony with the Word of God, though all the world stand against us.

Misunderstanding abounds even on relatively minor religious-liberty issues. Some Seventh-day Adventists want the government to sponsor prayer in public schools; other Adventists reject that idea as an infringement upon religious liberty. Some Adventists see Ronald Reagan as having done more to endanger religious freedom in America than any other president in history; while other Adventists voted for him—twice! And though some Adventists fear Jerry Falwell* as a man who could bring persecution, other Adventists send him money. Before his resignation, Falwell told a General

---

*Jerry Falwell, a fundamentalist minister, was the president of the Moral Majority, a conservative Protestant organization established to effect political change.

Conference vice-president that his third biggest financial supporters had been Seventh-day Adventists.

Clearly, we need a better understanding of the great truths we have been given. Is there a theological basis for religious liberty? What does the Bible say about religious liberty? What is the history of religious liberty in America? How is liberty best implemented? What forces are now in operation that jeopardize our liberty? What role will religious freedom play in last-day events? And, most important, what will God's remnant face when their religious freedom is wiped away and they confront the dragon's wrath?

Chapter 3

Jesus and Religious Liberty

From the time of the pioneers, Adventists have claimed the Bible as the basis of our faith. We have built an unshakable biblical foundation for the seventh-day Sabbath, the divinity of Christ, the investigative judgment—all our doctrines. Adventism is as firm as the Word of God itself.

But do we have a biblical basis for the principles of religious freedom? The Bible teaches that religious liberty will be inexorably woven into the tumult of the last days. Our families, freedom, even lives will be at risk by the stand we take regarding religious freedom. Is there a biblical basis for us to take such a position?

Of course. Shadrach, Meshach, and Abednego, three Hebrew boys in Babylon, refused to worship the golden image, though the law said that they must or die. Daniel, refusing to break the commandment about having other gods before the Lord, would not heed the "royal statute," which forbade praying to any except King Darius. The Bible sings with such stories, stories of God's faithful servants—those who were jailed, beaten, scourged, stoned, exiled, and slain rather than deny the true God. They all, with Peter, could exclaim, "We ought to obey God rather than men." Acts 5:29.

Yet the adventures in faith of Daniel, Shadrach, and Peter don't give us the entire picture of the religious liberty question. The moral of their stories is too easy, their message too clear. They are black-and-white prints in a four-color world.

Religious liberty is more than the right to worship God correctly. It is the right to worship God *incorrectly,* or even not at all. Religious liberty is the right to burn incense to Baal, to worship fire, to sacrifice chickens to Satan. True religious liberty is what St. Augustine condemned as "the liberty of self-ruin," the right to be wrong, so wrong that you will burn in hell.

This liberty is what the Bible teaches.

The cross of Jesus Christ is the greatest example of God's conception of religious liberty. The Creator of the universe, hanging bloody between heaven and earth, displayed the sanctity of free choice before humanity—even all the universe. The Son of God hung, nailed by His hands and feet, a crown of thorns upon His head—because He gave mankind the choice whether or not to serve Him. Jesus Christ was crucified because He allowed us religious freedom.

Had God not created man with that capacity to choose, man would not have sinned, God's law would not have been broken, death would not have come, and Jesus Christ would not have had to die.

"To deprive man of the freedom of choice would be to rob him of his prerogative as an intelligent being, and make him a mere automaton. It is not God's purpose to coerce the will. Man was created a free moral agent."—*Patriarchs and Prophets*, pages 331, 332.

Because Jesus deemed our religious freedom so sacred, so fundamental to His universe—He Himself paid the penalty for the wrong choices our freedom could bring. Rather than to force us not to sin, He became "sin for us." 2 Corinthians 5:21. Rather than curse us by making us mere automatons, He became a "curse for us." Galatians 3:13. Rather than make us live without free choice, He "died for us" instead. Romans 5:8.

"Why did God allow this fearful iniquity that man might be made free? To this there is but one answer. It was because He knew the worthlessness of all forced obedience, and therefore, the freedom to sin was absolutely necessary for the possibility of righteousness."—*Watchman*, May 1, 1906.

God's dealing with Adam in Eden displays the principles of true religious freedom. God said to Adam, "Of the tree of the knowledge of good and evil, thou shalt not eat of it: for in the day that thou eatest thereof thou shalt surely die." Genesis 2:17.

That the Lord had to tell Adam not to eat of the tree shows that the capacity to choose was created in him from the start. As the Lord molded Adam from the dust of the earth, He crafted into the infinite web of his brain the ability to choose right and wrong. Had the ability not been wired in, God would have had no need to warn him against a wrong choice Adam could not have made.

The tree of the knowledge of good and evil was within Adam's reach, within the grasp of his hands. If the tree were on the moon or on another planet out of his reach, or had God first placed that cherubim with a flaming sword before it, He would have had no reason to warn the man about eating from it, any more than a father has a reason to warn his three-year-old not to fly to Pluto. Instead, God created in Adam the ability to choose evil and then allowed him to act upon that choice.

God, obviously, felt that freedom of choice is so fundamental, that He would not infringe upon it—no matter the consequences. He knew the risks. He knew that war and disease and famine and death could rack His creation. Most important, He knew that using that free choice man would eventually choose to nail Him to a cross. Yet God allowed man freedom anyway, and because the first Adam abused that freedom, the second Adam had to come: "As by the offence of one judgment came upon all men to condemnation; even so by the righteousness of one the free gift came upon all men unto justification of life. For as by one man's disobedience many were made sinners, so by the obedience of one shall many be made righteous." Romans 5:18, 19.

Free choice is not confined to man or to the earth; it is a universal principle of all creation. How could Lucifer, the covering cherub, have rebelled, unless God gave him the capacity to choose evil and then allowed him to act upon that choice?

"Thus saith the Lord; Thou sealest up the sum, full of wisdom, and perfect in beauty. Thou hast been in Eden the garden of God; every precious stone was thy covering. . . . Thou art the anointed cherub that covereth; and I have set thee so: . . . thou hast walked up and down in the midst of the stones of fire. Thou wast perfect in all thy ways from the day that thou wast created, till iniquity was found in thee." Ezekiel 28:12-15.

Satan was the "anointed cherub," the most glorious and powerful angel in heaven—and created perfect. Perfection, then, obviously included free choice, the ability to choose— even evil. "Thou has said, . . . I will exalt my throne above the stars of God: I will sit also upon the mount of the congregation: . . . I will ascend above the heights of the clouds; I will be like the most High." Isaiah 14:13, 14.

Satan became proud, exalted, jealous, not because God created him that way, but because God gave him free choice, and Satan made the wrong ones. He slandered God, plotted against Him, and worked to overthrow His government—all within heaven itself! And because it was against His principle to force the will of any of His creatures, God didn't stop him. Instead, He begged him to repent. "God in His great mercy bore long with Lucifer," Ellen White explains (*The Great Controversy*, page 495), and He tried to persuade Satan to end his rebellion. Yet the mighty angel refused, and God would not force Satan into compliance, any more than He forced Adam not to eat of the tree.

Satan persuaded other angels to rebel. Even though God could have blotted them out in a flash or created them so they could not choose evil or so restricted them that they could not act upon their wrong choices—He instead allowed them to foment an open rebellion in heaven itself!

"There was war in heaven: Michael and his angels fought against the dragon; and the dragon fought and his angels, and prevailed not; neither was their place found any more in heaven." Revelation 12:7.

Religious freedom is found throughout the cosmos, wherever the principles of God reign. In *Early Writings,* pages 39, 40, Ellen White wrote of a planet shown to her in vision. She described its inhabitants as "noble, majestic, and lovely. And they bore the express image of Jesus." She then spoke to one, asking why they were "so much more lovely than those on the earth." The reply: "We have lived in strict obedience to the commandments of God, and have not fallen by disobedience, like those on the earth." Then she saw two trees. "The fruit of both looked beautiful, but of one they could not eat. They had power to eat of both, but were forbidden to eat of one. Then my attending angel said to me, 'None in this place have tasted of the forbidden tree; but if they should eat, they would fall.' "

Here, too, God's great principles of religious freedom are manifest. The inhabitants are forbidden to eat of one of the trees. Why did God have to forbid them? Obviously because they had the freedom to choose to eat of it, otherwise God would not have bothered to make the prohibition. They also had "power to eat of both."

Again, God gave His creation not only free choice, but

power to act upon that choice. Unlike Satan and Adam, though, these extraterrestrials made the right one.

No wonder, then, that when upon the earth Jesus never forced anyone to follow Him. Jesus didn't give man freedom of choice, only to later trample on that freedom Himself, or to appoint some ecclesiastical or civil power to trample upon it instead. Force is contrary to the principles of His government. Jesus desired only the service of love, which can never come by force. Only by love is love awakened.

For three and a half years Jesus straightened the gnarled bones of cripples, raised to life those reeking in death, opened dark eyes to light, silent ears to sound, and filled deflated souls with words of hope. He wanted people to follow Him because of an intelligent appreciation of who He was and what He represented. He sought to win people only by the power of love, through the Spirit of God working on their hearts. Any other kind of allegiance was worthless; that was why Jesus said that the most important commandment was "to love the Lord thy God with all thy heart, with all thy soul, and with all thy mind."

At first vast multitudes followed Jesus in His earthly ministry. Having tasted the fish and the loaves, they hoped for riches, glory, and power. Eventually, when they realized that they might get nothing more than fish and loaves from Jesus in this life, they abandoned Him. Why? Because their faith was not based on love. And if their faith, based on hope of earthly gain, proved so weak and worthless that they would abandon Jesus, how much more worthless is a faith that comes only by coercion, either from the barrel of a gun or from a state decree? Get a bigger gun or change the decree, and the religion will change accordingly. Remove the gun, annul the decree, and the faith will prove as fleeting as a bullet, as fragile as paper.

Jesus promised freedom from sin, guilt, condemnation—but He never forced that freedom upon anyone, for coercion was just another form of the bondage that He came to free us from. He, better than any, knew the fearful consequences of disobedience. Nevertheless, He allowed men to disobey, reject, and finally kill Him, even though by so doing they would bring ruin upon themselves, their families, their nation.

The rich young ruler asked Jesus about what he needed to do to be saved. Jesus told him, and the man walked away. Jesus knew the consequences of that decision. He loved the young ruler, but He didn't stop him. Never did Jesus defy the sanctity of free will. He pleaded, wept, admonished—but never forced.

Just because He didn't coerce doesn't mean that Jesus taught universalism, that everyone will be saved, or that all faiths are merely different paths to the Father. "I am the way, the truth, and the life," He said (John 14:6); "no man cometh unto the Father, but by me." Jesus warned that disobedience would bring death. He warned the Jews about hell, judgment, and the wages of sin, just as He warned Lucifer in heaven, Adam in Eden, and the inhabitants of the other worlds—just as He warns us today. Yet He still allows us to make our own choices, just as He allowed Adam, Lucifer, and the inhabitants of the other worlds.

How ironic, too, because if anyone had the right to force obedience, it was Jesus. He was God, the Creator of the universe, the great I AM. He created Lucifer, the angels, the planets, and Adam. He gave them form, substance, intelligence, and life. All that they are, were, or ever could be came from Jesus. He deserves obedience, praise, and worship, yet He never compels any to give that obedience, praise, or worship. It must come only by free choice.

Two centuries ago, Thomas Jefferson, understanding this principle of religious freedom, said that God, though "being

Lord both of body and mind, yet chose not to propagate it [religion] by coercions on either, as was in His Almighty power to do." Jefferson also warned about "fallible and uninspired men" who assume "dominion over the faith of others, setting up their own opinions and modes of thinking as the only true and infallible" and then endeavor "to impose them on others."

If God Himself will not force obedience, even at the cost of the cross—then how dare we?

Unfortunately, from the beginning of history, men have dared. And many still do.

Chapter 4

The American Tragedy

America is heading for tragedy. The Bible says it, through prophetic gift Ellen White says it, and those who know where to look can see it. National apostasy, we are told, will bring national ruin. America will cast shadows where it once beamed light. The nation that preached religious liberty will practice religious tyranny. The lamb will speak as a dragon.

"I beheld another beast coming up out of the earth; and he had two horns like a lamb, and he spake like a dragon." Revelation 13:11.

Who does a dragon represent? "The great dragon was cast out, that old serpent, called the Devil, and Satan, which deceiveth the whole world." Revelation 12:9.

The dragon symbolizes Satan. America, then, will speak, will act, like Satan, at least in regard to religious freedom, because religious freedom is the issue in this part of Revelation.

How does Satan act in regard to religious liberty? The Bible has the answer, and it is found in what might seem the unlikeliest part of the Bible: the book of Job.

Indeed, one of the great issues in Job revolved around worship. Would Job worship God, despite great pressure not to? One of the great issues in the last days will revolve around worship too. Will there be a people who worship God, despite great pressure not to?

God has called out a people, to "worship him that made

27

heaven, and earth, and the sea, and the fountains of waters." Revelation 14:7. Other forces will unite to enforce not the worship of God, but "the beast and his image." Just as in Job, the issue is Will people worship the true God, the Creator? And just as in Job, the devil will throw all his weight into the effort to make them abandon God. They, too, might lose their homes, servants, possessions, because economic pressure will be brought upon them. "No man might buy or sell, save he that had the mark, or the name of the beast, or the number of his name." Revelation 13:17. Like Job, their families could be killed. And like Job, they might suffer great physical pain. All these things will be brought upon them for the exact same reason they were brought upon Job: to turn them away from worshiping God.

And yet, what did God do to keep Job on His side? Did God threaten Job? Did He say, "If you think the devil is doing a number on you, turn away from Me and I will make things worse for you"? Of course not. Satan might use coercion, but not God: "God never forces the will or the conscience; but Satan's constant resort—to gain control of those whom he cannot otherwise seduce—is compulsion by cruelty. Through fear or force he endeavors to rule the conscience and to secure homage to himself."—*The Great Controversy,* page 591.

Indeed, the devil uses force, violence, deceit, anything to coerce the will, to bend the conscience, to break men into compliance with his lies, for he "was a liar from the beginning." According to Revelation 13:11, these methods will be utilized by America.

It won't, of course, be the first time a nation has used violence to coerce religious belief. Whether in the Orient or the Occident, in BC or AD, whether Christian or heathen, white or black, civilized or savage, men have persecuted others for religious purposes. "Never in civilization," wrote historian Theodore White, "had there been any state that left each individual to find his way to God without the guidance of the state."

And to help people find their way, the state has employed the rack, the sword, the dungeon, and terror. "It is, indeed, better that men should be brought to serve God by instruction than by fear of punishment, or by pain," said St. Augustine. "But because the former means are better, the latter must not therefore be neglected."[1]

Augustine wouldn't have been disappointed. Men have beaten, blinded, jailed, humiliated, threatened, starved, beheaded, hanged, burned, whipped, mauled, and drowned men, women, and children—usually in order to lead them to God and eternal bliss.

"It would be almost unbelievable, if history did not record the tragic fact," said Chief Justice Walter P. Stacy of the North Carolina Supreme Court, "that men have gone to war and cut each other's throats because they could not agree as to what was to become of them after their throats were cut."[2]

Throughout history, almost the whole world has used the devil's methods. And no wonder, for the Bible says that the devil "deceiveth the whole world." And according to Scripture, America is heading the same way.

Before it speaks as a dragon, though, America is described as a lamb. What does a lamb represent? "Behold the Lamb of God, which taketh away the sin of the world." John 1:29. "The lamb slain from the foundation of the world." Revelation 13:8. "He is brought as a lamb to the slaughter." Isaiah 53:7. The lamb represents Jesus of Nazareth, and Revelation uses that symbol to describe America in the context of religious freedom.

It fits. Jesus didn't force people to follow any religion, and neither does America. Jesus didn't use violence to coerce religious compliance, and neither does America. Jesus didn't use the state to enforce His beliefs, and neither does America.

Jesus allowed people free choice, and so does America. Jesus gave people a wonderful opportunity to learn truth, and so does America. Jesus allowed people the right to be wrong, and so does America. In short, as far as the important question of religious liberty is concerned, America has indeed been Christlike.

America, though, wasn't always lamblike. Prior to the Revolution and the ratifying of the Constitution, a dragon, more than a lamb, would have better symbolized America. A glimpse of America's past will help reveal her future. Freedom of religion was the exception, not the rule. The colonies were not experiments in civil and religious liberties.

"Persecution," declared John Cotton of the Massachusetts Bay Colony, "is not wrong in itself; it is wicked for falsehood to persecute truth, but it is the sacred duty of truth to persecute falsehood."[3]

Cotton's attitude was in vogue, and truth persecuted falsehood in almost every colony. Truth, though, varied from colony to colony, and each one had strict rules regarding truth. Old Anglican Virginia, which eventually produced Thomas Jefferson, James Madison, George Washington, and Patrick Henry, had laws that required everyone to be a churchgoer (Anglican church) and to observe Sabbath (Sunday). Its laws called for the punishment of the blasphemous, sacrilegious, or those who criticized the doctrine of the Trinity. Penalties included the loss of a "dayes allowance," "whippings," "a bodkin thrust through his tongue," and six months in the "gallies." Offenses included missing divine services (held twice daily), Sabbath breaking, or refusing religious instruction. Heresy was considered a capital crime.

Maryland had a more liberal position of nondiscrimination in respect to "any person professing to believe in Jesus Christ." In 1649, the colony passed a law which provided toleration for all "professing to believe in Jesus Christ" and who do not deny the Trinity or the divinity of Jesus. Those opposing these teachings were to "be punished with death and confiscation . . . of all his or her lands."[4]

Religious freedom wasn't unheard of in the early Colonies. It was just applied differently. Nathaniel Ward of Massachusetts Bay said that "all Familists, Antinomians, Anabaptists, and other Enthusiasts, shall have free liberty to keep away from us, and such as will come to be gone as fast they can, the sooner the better."[5]

Sunday laws were rampant. People were jailed, whipped, and fined for breaking the "divine Sabbath." The Virginia Sunday law of 1610 required attendance at a "diuine service" twice that day, with economic fines for the first two offenses, and "to suffer death" for the third. In New England, church attendance was required, and one record tells of the "tithing man," who "entered private homes on the Sabbath and hustled out any loiters."[6]

People were forced to pay taxes to support the clergy of whichever denomination happened to be established in the area. As late as 1774, eighteen Baptists were jailed in Massachusetts for refusing to pay taxes for the support of their town's Congregational minister. Almost all the colonies had laws requiring the payment of taxes for the established church, even though those of other religions lived in the colonies. This situation caused bitterness, confusion, even violence.

In colonies with established churches, dissenters were banished, hounded, jailed, whipped, and persecuted. Jews, Quakers, and Catholics were hated and persecuted almost everywhere. In Boston, Quakers were hanged; in New York, Catholics were killed. Peter Stuyvesant, the Dutch governor of the New Netherlands, kept Jews from the retail trade, and throughout most of the colonies Jews were forbidden to vote or hold public office. Baptists, in early America a dissenting

Protestant group, were beaten by mobs, fined, and jailed for their religious beliefs. Persecution of local Baptists strongly influenced the thinking of James Madison. "That diabolical Hell-conceived principle of persecution," he wrote to a Philadelphia friend in 1774, "rages among some and to their eternal Infamy the Clergy can furnish their Quota of Imps for such business. This vexes me the most of any thing whatever. There are at this [time] in the adjacent County not less than 5 or 6 well meaning men in the close Goal [jail] for publishing their religion. Sentiments which in the main are very orthodox."[7]

As bad as America was, it was a vast improvement over Europe, which for centuries echoed with the cries of religious violence. Blood, sweat, and tears were spilled, dripped, and shed in America, but just a few drops compared to the rivers that ravaged Europe. In France, Spain, England, the Netherlands, Germany, Italy, millions massacred each other in the name of God.

The American colonies were spared the degree of violence—if for no other reason than that they didn't have as many people, or that there were so many different religious groups that none could get supremacy over all the colonies (not that some didn't try). Nevertheless, most colonies discriminated against minorities. They couldn't help it! When religion is established, it becomes the legal, official faith, and local laws will reflect that faith, laws that can—and inevitably do—conflict with the belief and practices of other persuasions. These people, by reason of religious conviction alone, must then necessarily break those laws that conflict with their faith, and thus face the consequences. Back then the consequences included fines, jail, having a "bodkin thrust through" their tongues, or even death.

"When the power, prestige, and financial support of government is placed behind a particular religious belief," said

Supreme Court Justice William Brennan, "the indirect coercive pressure upon religious minorities to conform to the prevailing officially approved religion is plain."

In 1776, Thomas Jefferson, attempting to bring religious freedom to Virginia, listed the restrictions still on the books. Heresy, a capital offense; denial of the Trinity or the divine authority of the Scriptures, punishable by imprisonment; Roman Catholics, excluded from civil posts; freethinkers and Unitarians, their children taken away. Though by the eve of the American Revolution many of these and similar laws were no longer enforced, either in Virginia or other colonies, most colonies still maintained religious establishments and, though resentful of the British violations of their rights, they violated the rights of Jews, Catholics, and dissenting Protestants.

After the incorporation of the Bill of Rights into the United States Constitution in 1791, however, religious discrimination was, at least officially, against the law. The government was not allowed to persecute or prohibit religious dissenters, nor make any religion official, because once a religion becomes official it almost inevitably results in persecution or discrimination of members of the "unofficial" faiths.

George Washington, in a peace treaty with Tripoli, declared that the "government of the United States of America is not, in any sense, founded on the Christian religion." Some Americans, though, insisted that it was. Massachusetts, for example, didn't completely annul "Christian" laws until 1833, and today, some claim that the Constitutional prohibition against establishing a religion (despite the Fourteenth Amendment) does not apply to individual states. In the early 1980s, for example, a District Court in Alabama ruled that the state had the right to promote a religious exercise in school because the Constitutional prohibition wasn't applicable to it (in 1985 the Supreme Court overturned that ruling).

When the Constitution was originally signed in 1787 in Philadelphia, it had only one clause that dealt with religion: Clause 3 of Article 6. Charles Pinckney, a delegate from South Carolina, proposed that "no religious test shall ever be required as a qualification to any office or public trust under the United States." This clause meant that no one could be denied an office in government because of his religious beliefs. This proposal represented a radical departure from custom. Pennsylvania required an officeholder to believe in one God and in a future reward and punishment. New York banned Catholics from state office. Maryland, New Hampshire, North Carolina, and Vermont barred everyone but Protestants from holding office. Pinckney's proposal, however, passed. Only North Carolina voted No (Maryland was "divided"). Maryland's Luther Martin declared that "in a Christian country it would be at least decent to hold out some distinction between the professors of Christianity and downright infidelity and paganism." A Massachusetts deposition warned that this clause "opened a door for Jews, Turks, and infidels."[8]

What the original Constitution in 1787 did not have, though, was the First Amendment, which forbade Congress from establishing a religion, or from passing any law that would prohibit the free exercise of religion. Many delegates, including James Madison, didn't want it written!

Indeed, the Constitution never gave the government authority to legislate religion. The only time the Constitution even mentioned religion was in Pinckney's clause, and even there it placed a *restriction* on the government. Therefore, Madison and others felt that the establishment and the free exercise clauses were unnecessary, superfluous, because the Constitution hadn't granted the government power to establish or prohibit a religion anyway. Why a Bill of Rights to prohibit what the government never had?

James Wilson of Pennsylvania, responding to the accusation that the Constitution didn't give adequate religious protection from government infringement, asked: "What part of this system puts it in the power of Congress to attack those rights? When there is no power to attack, it is idle to prepare the means of defense."[9] Though not dealing specifically with religion, Alexander Hamilton in *The Federalist* gave the basic principle: "For why declare that things shall not be done which there is no power to do? Why, for instance, should it be said that the liberty of the press shall not be restrained, when no power is given by which restrictions may be imposed?"

James Madison—as he spoke to the Virginia Convention in 1788, prior to its ratification of the Constitution—said it the clearest: "There is not a shadow of a right in the general government to intermeddle with religion."

Nevertheless, the failure to provide a Bill of Rights could have been the Achilles' heel of the Constitution. The Constitution might not have been ratified had not leaders like James Madison (who changed his mind) eventually promised to make a Bill of Rights as soon as the new government began to function. Too many Americans had suffered too much religious persecution not to want guaranteed protections. After the promise that a Bill of Rights would be forthcoming, eleven states voted to ratify the Constitution (North Carolina said No and independent Rhode Island didn't even bother calling a convention to consider it). This Constitution became the blueprint for the new national government of the United States of America.

Madison feared, however, that a Bill of Rights, which specifically denied powers that had not been granted to the government by the Constitution, could be construed to imply that the government had other powers that were not specifically mentioned in the Constitution either. For example, the Constitution does not give the government the right to legislate the hour Americans go to bed, any more than it gives it the right to legislate religion. Yet the Bill of Rights, which forbids the government to legislate religion, does not specifically forbid the government to legislate our bedtime. Does, then, the government have the right to tell us when to go to bed? Even though that right was not delegated to it in the general Constitution, it was not specifically denied to it in the Bill of Rights. Madison said that "if an enumeration be made of our rights, will it not be implied, that everything omitted, is given to the general government?"[10] As we will see in a later chapter, Madison's fears have been realized.

The Constitution, as far as religion is concerned, was designed to limit the government. In the entire document, including the Bill of Rights, religion is mentioned only twice, in Clause 3 of Article 6 and in the First Amendment. And both times the laws *restrict* the government in the area of religion.

Article 6, we saw, limits the government by not allowing it to discriminate, on the basis of religion, against anyone who wants to hold public office—a hefty limitation in those days.

The First Amendment reads that "Congress shall make *no law* respecting the establishment of religion or prohibiting the free exercise thereof." Here, too, religion is mentioned, and again the laws mentioning it restrict the government. The clause says that the Congress is not allowed to many *any* law regarding the establishment of religion, which means simply that the government isn't allowed to establish, form, or promote any type of sectarian belief. Though in other nations, the government promoted, paid for, and pushed the dogmas and beliefs of a certain religious system—this law was designed to keep the government from doing any such thing.

The next clause, which deals with the free exercise of religion, is also a restriction. It stops the government from prohibiting the free exercise of religion. All over the world, and even in the colonies, dissenting groups—usually those not part of the established religion—were hounded, persecuted, or forbidden to practice their religion by the government. The First Amendment forbade it from happening in America.

The only time religion is mentioned in the Constitution is to stop the government from making laws that would either establish, discriminate against, or prohibit it. If the government is not allowed to make laws regarding religion, then it will never be able to persecute or discriminate against on the basis of religion. Herein is the secret of America's great religious freedoms!

The First Amendment clauses are closely linked because the establishment of one religion is usually the first step toward the prohibition of others. Establish one religion, and the free exercise of another will be inhibited. This concept is important, especially in the light of recent thrusts to reinterpret the meaning of the Constitution, particularly the establishment clause, a reinterpretation that could ultimately undo its meaning, trash our religion-liberty safeguards, and open the way for America to speak as a dragon.

The Constitution—which ensures that the state won't wield too much influence in the churches, and the churches too much influence in the states—has made America the freest nation in the world. No wonder Massachusetts Baptist leader Isaac Backus said that the Constitution "opened for the establishment of righteous government, and for securing of equal liberty, as never before to any people on the earth."

Though designed to make the government "neutral" toward religion, these Constitutional prohibitions are really rooted in the New Testament. The New Testament does not openly teach the separation of church and state, but it does teach complete religious freedom, and separation of church and state has proved to be the best—if not the only way—to give complete religious freedom the way that Jesus gave, lived, and taught it. Far from being "hostile" to religion, particularly Christianity, or even "neutral" toward it (as it is supposed to be)—the Constitutional clauses regarding religious liberty are "Christian," which is why America, at least for the beginning of its history, is symbolized by a lamb.

No wonder Jerry Combee and Cline Hall, professors at Liberty Baptist College in Lynchburg, Virginia, wrote that the First Amendment was "no plot of atheistic conspirators, but the result of persevering Christians."[11]

"Indeed, without stretching very far," writes historian William Lee Miller, "one could claim that this broad river of history—let us call it dissenting Protestantism—had more to do, over all, over time, pound for pound, head for head, with the shaping of the American tradition religious liberty than did the rational Enlightenment."[12]

Unquestionably, Article 6 and the Free Exercise and Establishment clauses of the First Amendment, as simple and innocuous as they sound, have made America to be like the lamb depicted in Revelation 13. Yet eventually the lamb will make an image to the beast—and the only way America could, would be either to take away those two sections of the Constitution, trample on their meaning, or reinterpret them to mean something different.

"In order for the United States to form an image of the beast," wrote Ellen White, "the religious power must so control the civil government that the authority of the state will also be employed by the church to accomplish her own ends."—*The Great Controversy,* page 443.

The only way for the religious power to "so control the civil government" in America would be to get around these Constitutional restrictions. America will have some type of religious establishment, similar to that of the "beast"—the church-state system in Europe where the church controlled the government and used it to promote dogma and to persecute dissenters—and those who refuse to obey the laws of established religion and "worship the beast" will be persecuted.

For America, then, to fulfill its prophetic role, it must either abolish, annul, or reinterpret its principles of religious freedom. Something will lift the restrictions that till now have kept the government from legislating laws that could bring persecution.

As we will see, forces are working now to accomplish those ends. And, ultimately, one way or another, they will succeed.

---

1. Philip Schaff, *History of the Christian Church* (Grand Rapids, Mich.: William B. Eerdmans Publishing Company, 1950), vol. 3, section 27, pp. 144.

2. *State v. Beal,* 199 NC. 278, 302, (1930).

3. John Fiske, *Beginning of New England,* p. 178. In *American State Papers,* p. 231.

4. Anson Phelps Stokes, *Church and State in the United States* (New York: Harper and Brothers, 1950), vol. 1, pp. 189-191.

5. "The Simple Cobler of Aggawam . . . ," in Perry G. E. Miller and Thomas H. Johnson, eds., *The Puritans* (New York: American Book Co., 1938), p. 227.

6. "The Blue Laws of New England," *Liberty,* vol. 58 (1963), no. 1, pp. 18, 19.

7. William T. Hutchinson et al., eds, *The Papers of James Madison* (Chicago, 1962), I, p. 106.

8. Philip B. Kurland and Ralph Lerner, eds., *The Founder's Constitution* (Chicago: University of Chicago Press, 1987), vol. 4, p. 642.

9. Quoted in Levy, Leonard, *The Establishment Clause* (New York: MacMillian Publishing Company, 1986), p. 65.

10. Quoted in Levy, Leonard, p. 116.

11. Jerry Combee and Cline Hall, *Designed for Destiny* (Wheaton, Ill.: Tyndale House Publishers, Inc., 1985), p. 22.

12. William Lee Miller, *The First Liberty* (New York: Alfred A. Knopf, 1986), p. 153.

Chapter 5

People of the Beast

Nothing should put more fire into Adventist blood than the appearance of the New Christian Right in American politics. That this wing of American Christianity should, in less than a decade, rise from the bowels of political impotency into the heart of the American conservative movement is nothing but prophetic. No other power on earth has such potential to make America speak like a dragon.

Almost two thousand years ago, Jesus warned that "it is not everyone who keeps saying to me, 'Lord, Lord' who will enter the kingdom of Heaven, but the man who actually does my Heavenly Father's will.

"In 'that day' many will say to me, 'Lord, Lord, didn't we preach in your name, didn't we cast out devils in your name, and do many great things in your name?' Then I shall tell them plainly, 'I have never known you. Go away from me, you have worked on the side of evil.'" Matthew 7:21-23, Phillips.

Who was Jesus warning? Was it atheists, agnostics, Communists, infidels, secular humanists, Muslims, Jews, Rastafarians, or Buddhists?

Not likely. Atheists, agnostics, infidels, etc., don't say, "Lord, Lord," nor cast out demons in Jesus' name. *Christians do*—yet Jesus warned that "many" of them will be "on the side of evil."

Jesus learned by personal experience: one of His own disciples—someone who said, "Lord, Lord," and who had cast out demons in His name—betrayed Him.

In the parable of the wheat and the tares, Jesus taught that false Christians would continue to infiltrate the church until His second coming. Paul cautioned that after his departing, "shall grievous wolves enter in among you." Acts 20:29. Peter warned about false prophets and teachers within the church who "privily shall bring in damnable heresies." 2 Peter 2:1. The Bible teaches clearly the disquieting concept that evil believers will infest the church until the end of the world.

"Wherefore ye be witnesses unto yourselves, that ye are the children of them which killed the prophets," Jesus said to the church of His day. "I send unto you prophets, and wise men, and scribes: some of them ye shall kill and crucify; and some of them shall ye scourge in your synagogues, and persecute them from city to city: that upon you may come all the righteous blood shed upon the earth, from the blood of righteous Abel unto the blood of Zacharias son of Barachias, whom ye slew between the temple and the altar. . . . O Jerusalem, Jerusalem, thou that killest the prophets." Matthew 23:31, 34-37.

Jesus wasn't talking to sun-worshiping Babylonians, child-sacrificing Moabites, or self-immolating heathens. He was talking to the "church," which fulfilled His prediction of bloodshed and apostasy, culminating at Calvary.

As the gospel went to the Gentiles, the church was so corrupted by the tares Jesus predicted, the grievous wolves described by Paul, and the false teachers warned of by Peter that the great biblical truths of salvation were lost in a blitz of paganism, idolatry, and error. Those who adhered to the Bible were accused of heresy, blasphemy, and sedition. They were hunted, exiled, branded, tortured, and slain—all in an attempt to eradicate truth from the earth.

Here, too, their persecutors were not the Ottoman Turks, Attila the Hun, or the Nordic Vikings. *It was, again, the church!*

No question, God's truth faces challenges. Communism presents a grave danger to America and Christianity. Lenin had said that "thousands of natural catastrophes and epidemics are preferable to the slightest notion of God." Marx had said, "The idea of God is the keynote of a perverted civilization. It must be destroyed." Khrushchev had said: "If anyone believes our smiles involve abandonment of the teaching of Marx, Engels, and Lenin, he deceives himself. Those who wait for that must wait until a shrimp learns to whistle."

Despite everything hostile in Communism, despite its persecution of Christians, its disdain for religion and for the freedoms that America espouses—Communism does not present the threat that the Bible and spirit of prophecy warn about.

Despite the growing militancy of Islam, despite its violent nationalism and jingoism, despite its menacing presence in the world and its hostility to religious freedom—militant Islam is not the biblical threat.

Despite the contamination of secularism and materialism, despite the advancement of secular humanism and its bogus notions of humanity, despite its situational ethics and corrupting influence in our society, especially public schools— secularism is not the threat the Bible or spirit of prophecy warn about.

Instead, as in the past, the danger will come from the church itself!

Enter the New Christian Right.

Centuries ago, when the Christian church formed an illicit union with the Roman Empire, they gave birth to an illegitimate child, a beast with "seven heads and ten horns." Revelation 13:1. America, by uniting church and state, will form an "image" to this beast. Not a perfect copy, not a precise replica—but an "image," something that resembles the earlier church-state union between Christianity and the government.

To see how America, by uniting church and state, could form an "image" to the beast, we need to look at how the church and state united to form the original beast to see if any parallels exist.

"When the early church became corrupted by departing from the simplicity of the gospel and accepting heathen rites and customs," Ellen White wrote, "she lost the Spirit and power of God; and in order to control the consciences of the people, she sought the support of the secular power."—*The Great Controversy,* page 443.

The early church, she said, became corrupted by false teaching, rites, and customs. It had compromised with error. The churches were part Christian, part pagan. They would pray to Jesus, but then bow to a great Babylonian "mother goddess" in the form of Mary. Plato's immortal souls became dogma; the pagan Sunday became the Sabbath. Local church authority was replaced by ecclesiastical authoritarianism at the hands of a single official, the bishop. The Bible was hidden from view, replaced by the tradition of the church. Indeed, the longer the church was in power, the greater were her errors.

What about the "church" today, those seeking the power of the state? Is it doctrinally pure, or has it, like the early church, been corrupted with false teaching?

Jerry Falwell used to brag about how his organization was composed of Protestants, Catholics, Jews, and Mormons. We know that the Catholics, Jews, and Mormons have major theological errors. But what about the doctrines of the Protestants, the majority of those who compose the New Right and who want to make America a "Christian" nation or, in their more careful vernacular, to bring "Judeo-Christian" values back to America?

The first problem is: many of their own doctrines and beliefs aren't even Judeo, much less Christian!

They all keep, one way or another, Sunday—a day that has no authority in the Old or New Testaments, but is a holdover from Roman sun worship. They have accepted the pagan doctrines of the immortality of the soul and an eternal-burning hell. Pat Robertson, who wants to restore America to her original "Judeo-Christian roots," said that the spirit of man at death "goes into an everlasting state, because spirits are immortal and cannot die." Using the parable of the rich man and Lazarus, Robertson asserts that "the Bible does not teach soul sleep." For Robertson, hell "consists of eternal and unending anguish apart from God and all that is good,"[1] while "those who are consigned to hell will be put out into the inky blackness of eternity, with nobody to turn to, nobody to talk to, and they will be constantly alone."[2]

Almost all Protestants in the New Right are futurists, accepting, in one form or another, the counter-reformation theology that identifies the antichrist as some unknown individual (Jimmy Swaggart thinks he will be a "Syrian Jew") who will arise in the last days and persecute the Jews in Palestine prior to the great Battle of Armageddon, which will result in the death of millions of Jews and the conversion to Christianity of the rest. Figures ranging from Guru Maharaj Ji to Henry Kissinger have come under suspicion as being the dreaded antichrist.

Many Protestants believe a doctrine of "once saved, always saved." They hold that once a person accepts Jesus Christ as his Saviour he can never lose his salvation, no matter how far he backslides. He can turn to crime, drugs, rape, even murder, but he's on his way to eternal bliss with Jesus in heaven.

Almost all in the New Right assume that Jesus will set up His millennial kingdom on the earth. "The millenium," says Robertson, "will be a time when Jesus Christ will reign as king, and the kingdom of God will be established on earth."[3] They believe that because Jesus died on the cross, pigs and lobsters and crabs are now clean. Many in the New Right, including Falwell, teach the pre-tribulation rapture, a time coming soon when suddenly all of God's faithful people will vanish. They will be driving in cars, sitting in restaurants, home watching television, when—poof!—they will be taken to heaven, nothing remaining of them except, says Jerry Falwell, "their clothes."

Just as when the church first linked with the state, American Christianity today festers with corruption, false doctrines, and unbiblical traditions. Because of these errors, the early church lost the power of the Spirit of God, which is why it grasped hold of the state instead. Could this same accusation be made about the American church today?

In 1984, a letter to the editor of *Time* magazine (October 8, 1984) said: "The ominous move by Evangelicals and Roman Catholics to intimidate the Government into enacting denominational dogma into public law is a crushing admission of failure by their clergy. It spotlights the inability of these ministers to persuade their own congregations to conform to church doctrine."

Though Falwell and others see this surge of political activism in the churches as a sign of "moral and spiritual rebirth for this country," the rise of the New Right and the sudden thrust of Christians into the political arena indicates a church that has *lost* the power of God's Spirit. Unable to "control the consciences" of the people, it seeks the "support of the secular power" instead. Indeed, just as in the formation of the original beast, the church today needs Caesar to do the things of God.

"Since we have failed to bring about a Jonah-like revival of repentance and a change in the hearts of men," says evangelist David Wilkerson, in an article criticizing the church's political thrust, "we will, according to some, take over the reins of government and legislate righteousness."

Their own words betray this spiritual impotency. "Many Christians are praying for and expecting revival," said New Right leader Tim LaHaye. "While it is true that God has already given America three national revivals in the past, we desperately need another one today. Personally, I am not sure we can have one without legislative reform."[4]

Since when was a spiritual revival dependent upon legislative reform? Imagine Peter at Pentecost, bemoaning the legislative ills in Jerusalem, much less Rome, and insisting that no cloven tongues of fire will fall from heaven until the government passes laws more akin to Christian theology. Spiritual revival is about as dependent upon legislative reform as NATO forces are on Wonder Woman. LaHaye's statement is indicative of a church so devoid of God that it needs Caesar instead. "It is error alone," said Thomas Jefferson, "which needs the support of government."

Pat Robertson, in his book *America's Dates with Destiny,* says that evangelicals will "have to change their *political* ways before they can change the ways of the nation." Italics supplied.[5] Change their political ways? What about their moral and spiritual ways through the Holy Spirit working in their lives, the way the Bible teaches? That Robertson, LaHaye, and other Christian leaders see the state as the necessary vehicle for Christians to bring moral change to the country is an admission of spiritual failure.

"We have disobeyed our Lord," said Bill Bright of Campus Crusade for Christ. "We have ceased to be the 'salt of the earth' and the 'light of the world,' as Christ has commanded. As a result, the moral fiber of America is rotting away—and our priceless freedom is in grave jeopardy."[6]

Two thousand years ago, when the church was small and the closest thing to mass communication was shouting from a rooftop, Christians exuded so much spiritual power—in politically hostile environment!—that their enemies declared: they "have turned the world upside down." Acts 17:6.

Today in America, despite millions and millions of Christians, despite more ordained ministers than the rest of the world combined, more Christian radio and television programs than the rest of the world combined, despite the highest church attendance in the world, and despite 80 million Americans who claim to be born again, including two past presidents—"American society seems as unaffected by Christian values," said Haddon Robinson in *Christianity Today* (January 17, 1986), "as the National Football League is by Sunday church services." Apparently, the salt has lost its savor.

Pollster George Gallup's massive poll of American Christianity in 1984 explains why. There exists, he wrote, "very little difference in the behavior of the churched and unchurched on a wide range of items including lying, cheating, and pilferage."[7]

Very little difference in the behavior of the churched and unchurched? Jesus said, "Be ye therefore perfect," yet many of His professed followers today are no less inclined to lie and cheat than unbelievers? Gallup's survey is a blistering condemnation of a people who are to be "perfecting holiness in the fear of God." 2 Corinthians 7:1. And many of these same people talk about "getting America right with God"?

Before his fall from grace amid charges of adultery, homosexuality, and financial shenanigans, the Reverend Jim

Bakker, for example, spent $120,000 on a political consultant to advise him on how he could involve himself in politics—no doubt also to help bring morality to America.

Gallup revealed why Christians scored so dismally: Many, he wrote, were "willing to make sacrifices up to a certain point on behalf of our faith, but we will go only so far."[8]

Jesus said that "whosoever he be of you that forsaketh not all that he hath, he cannot be my disciple." Luke 14:33. In the early church, those willing to forsake all for Jesus were hounded, persecuted, exiled, and killed. The rest—willing only "to make sacrifices up to a certain point"—they became the people of the beast.

A tract published by Tim LaHaye's American Coalition for Traditional Values admits that the Christian church has not been the moral example it should be: "While it is true that our primary job is to be the 'light of the world,' we are also commanded by our Lord to be the 'salt of the earth.' The moral decline of the past thirty years indicates we have not been the 'salt' to our society that our forefathers were."[9]

What answer did the ACTV tract provide? Personal repentance? Forsaking of sin? A spiritual revival among the churches? A return to apostolic godliness? An individual recommitment to Jesus?

Hardly. Instead, Christians become "salt" by the following: "establish a political action committee (PAC)," "encourage and preach on Christian activism," "organize a Good Government committee," "circulate petitions and lobby," "conduct political forums," "introduce candidates at services," and "pass out voting records and candidate surveys."[10]

No question, some Christians now involved in the New Right will side with those who "keep the commandments of God" when the real issues surface. But the majority won't. They never have, which is why God's people are described as a "remnant."

Other parallels exist between the formation of the first beast and what is happening today as the New Right seeks to bring church and state together in America. Early pagan emperors, particularly Constantine (under whose reign church and state originally united) needed the church for political purposes. "Therefore, that I may enjoy a happy life and reign," said Constantine, "I will . . . join myself to the cause of the Christians, who are growing daily, while the heathen are diminishing."[11]

Constantine brought Christians into the highest levels of government. "He called Christians," wrote historian Andrew Alflodi, "in ever-increasing numbers to the higher administrative posts of the Empire."[12]

According to historian Schaff, Constantine was "concerned more to advance the outward social position of the Christian religion, than to further its inward mission."[13]

Constantine believed that he had a call to save his people from destruction: "When godlessness, far and wide, lay heavy on men, when the State was threatened by the deadly pestilence of utter corruption and a radical cure was the urgent need, what a relief, what a salvation from the mischief did God contrive! . . . God decreed my service and accounted me fit to execute His decree."[14]

Constantine did enact needed laws that, according to historian Schaff "breathed the spirit of Christian justice and humanity." Constantine abolished crucifixion, forbade the branding of people in the face, ordered that prisoners awaiting trial should be given light and fresh air, and stopped gladiatorial games. He passed "pro-family" decrees that helped stopped infanticide (a common practice when parents had children they didn't want or couldn't care for), kept slave families together, and that helped widows, orphans, and minors. He enacted laws that protected female chastity, prohibited illicit intercourse, forbade the cohabitation of a concubine with a married man, and severely limited divorce, which was freely practiced under pagan Roman rule.

According to Eusebius, Constantine decreed that his non-Christian soldiers, those "who were as yet ignorant of divine truth," be paraded to a field every Sunday and ordered to offer a prayer, which Constantine himself prescribed, thanking God for "past benefits" and beseeching Him for "future blessings."[15]

Constantine believed that they had a divine mandate to rule the nation. Constantine gave the churches government money, erected "Christian symbols," and even made the world's first national Sunday law.

In the early phases of his reign, Constantine made numerous promises of religious liberty: "and that it was proper that the Christians, and all others, should have liberty to follow that mode of religion which to each of them seemed best. . . . For it befits the well-ordered state, and the tranquillity of our times that each individual be allowed, according to his own choice, to worship the Divinity."[16] He said also that "liberty is to be denied to no one, . . . but that to each one freedom is to be given to devote his mind to that religion which he may think himself adapted."[17]

Unfortunately, by establishing "Christianity," Constantine brought about the inevitable: the persecution of non-Christians. By claiming that the immorality of pagan religious practices was detrimental to the empire, he moved against pagan temples, pagan sacrifices, divination, astrology, and magic. Despite his promises of religious freedom, he initiated a systematic campaign to eradicate paganism, a campaign that his successors continued.

Constantine didn't, however, stop with paganism. Eventually, he persecuted unorthodox Christians as well. In an imperial edict against heretical Christians, he warned: "All ye who devise and support heresies by means of your private assemblies, with what a tissue of falsehood and vanity, with what destructive and venomous errors, your doctrines are inseparably interwoven. . . . All your counsels are opposed to the truth, but familiar with deeds of baseness. . . . We have directed, accordingly, that you be deprived of all the houses in which you are accustomed to hold your assemblies."[18] Of course, as the years progressed and the beast grew in power, this policy continued, and "unorthodox" Christians were soon deprived, not just of their houses—but of their lives, which is why the beast is described in the Bible as making "war with the saints." Daniel 7:21; Revelation 13:7.

During the 1980s in America, as in Constantine's empire, many politicians joined themselves to "the cause of the Christians"—for the same reason as Constantine: political expediency. Polls indicate that 40 percent of American adults claim to be born again. Add to them 50 million Catholics, give them a common cause, and they could dominate American politics for the rest of the century. Though Christians are far from politically homogenous, they nevertheless possess incredible political potential. "With two-thirds of America's population belonging to a religious body and 94 percent of our citizens professing a belief in God," said New Right activist Vern McLellan, "the vast Judeo-Christian bloc should be the most influential force in our country."[19] Historian Martin Marty says that the New Christian Right, after coming almost out of nowhere, now holds "the most visible and assertive political position in American religion."[20] No wonder that after 1984, the New Right showed such clout that "every declared Republican Presidential candidate openly sought its support."[21]

Just as in Constantine's day, Christians are being brought into the government in increasing numbers either on county, state, and federal levels. Just before the 1984 election, Jerry Falwell called on Americans to observe a National Day of

Fasting and Prayer to help insure that "religious men and women will be elected to public office on election day."[22] Said Pat Robertson during the election: "We're asking for Godly people to be in office . . . men and women who love God, who believe in the Bible, who have a principle. . . . These are the kind of people we want in office."[23] Perhaps the trend toward "Christianizing" the state was best expressed by White House associate liaison director Carold Sundseth, who told White House staffers to "get saved or get out."

The New Christian Right, despite all its talk about revival, is advancing only the outward, political, and social position of the church, as did Constantine. Politics will never advance the gospel in the heart of men. Jesus never tried to instill the gospel by politics, Constantine didn't, and the New Right can't—no matter how hard it tries.

Also, the New Christian Right believes, as did Constantine, that the welfare of the nation depends on them. "The issue is survival," said Jerry Falwell. "We must return to these [biblical] principles, as a nation, if we are to survive."[24] One New Christian Right organization called Christian Voice, appealing for funds, warned that donations "may well be the difference between America surviving and America being destroyed by God's wrath—perhaps through nuclear fire and brimstone."[25] In his book *Saints and Dirty Politics* Richard Hogue said that "if our country survives—and I realize that's a big IF—it will be because there is an awakening in the lives of committed Christians across our nation who finally begin to realize that it is not only their opportunity but also their absolute responsibility to be intricately involved in the political process of our country and use that involvement to turn this nation once again to the Lord."

A look at the New Christian Right agenda reveals that, like Constantine, they would enact some good laws. They, too, want laws to stop infanticide (now in the form of abortion), they, too, want laws that would increase morality, they, too, want laws that would protect the family. Indeed, like Constantine, much of what the New Christian Right envisions would be good for the nation.

Unfortunately, like Constantine, they want laws enforcing prayer. The New York Regent's Prayer, which the school board directed the children to recite, was similar to the prayer that Constantine wrote for his heathen soldiers. Both were prayers acknowledging dependence upon God, thanking Him for His blessings—and both were legislated. Like Constantine, the New Christian Right wants religious symbols on public property, they want government funds for their schools, and you don't need much imagination to see them pushing for a national Sunday law.

The New Christian Right talks about "religious freedom." So did Constantine—at least at first. Eventually, though, for the good of the empire, he rooted out "false" religions. Today the New Right has declared war against "religion of secular humanism," which is to them what paganism was to Constantine: a false, non-Christian, and immoral religion. Said Falwell: "It's Christ against humanism."[26]

Yet Constantine didn't end with the pagans, any more than the New Right will end with secular humanists. "The Falwells and Robertsons may settle for a watered-down state-endorsed religion for the time being," warns church-state expert Dr. Stan Hastey. "But in the long haul, what they seek is a state dominated by the orthodox. And they will decide what is orthodox."[27]

Indeed, the Bible makes it plain: Christians—not pagans, secular humanists, nor atheists—will be the persecuted group: "The dragon was wroth with the woman, and went to make war with the remnant of her seed, which keep the commandments of God, and have the testimony of *Jesus Christ.*" Revelation 12:17. Italics supplied.

Of course, twentieth-century America is not fourth-century Rome. The church of modern America is not the church of ancient Rome. The politics then is not the politics of today.

But then, again, America doesn't become the beast—just its image.

---

1. Pat Robertson, *Pat Robertson Answers* (New York: Thomas Nelson Publishers, 1984), p. 62.

2. *Ibid.,* p. 160.

3. *Ibid.,* p. 160.

4. Quoted in Vern McLellan, *Christians in the Political Arena* (Charlotte, N.C.: Associated Press, 1986), p. 162.

5. New York: Thomas Nelson Publishers, 1986, p. 299.

6. McLellan, p. 121.

7. *Religion in America,* Report No. 222, March 1984, p. 1.

8. *Ibid.,* p. 9.

9. "What a Church Can and Cannot Do Politically," published by American Coalition for Traditional Values, Washington, D.C.

10. *Ibid.*

11. Philip Schaff, *History of the Christian Church* (Grand Rapids, Mich.: Wm. B. Eerdmans Co., 1902), vol. 3, p. 20.

12. Andrew Alflodi, *The Conversion of Constantine and Pagan Rome* (London: Oxford University Press, 1948), p. 49.

13. Schaff, p. 17.

14. Quoted in Alflodi, p. 33.

15. Eusebius, "Church History," book X, chap. v. in *Nicene and Post-Nicene Fathers,* second series, vol. 1, p. 379.

16. "Decree of Nicomedia," quoted in Huttmann, Maude, *Establishment of Christianity and Proscription of Paganism* (New York: AMS Press, 1967), pp. 394, 395.

17. Eusebius, "Church History," book X, chap. v, in *Nicene and Post-Nicene Fathers,* pp 379.

18. Eusebius, "The Life of the Blessed Emperor Constantine," book III, chaps. lxix, lxv, in *Nicene and Post-Nicene Fathers,* vol. 1, p. 539.

19. McLellan, p. 113.

20. Martin Marty, "Transpositions: American Religion in the 1980s," Wade Clark Rood, ed., *Religion in America Today;* Annals of the American Academy of Political and Social Science (Beverly Hills, Calif.: Sage Publications, 1985), vol. 480, p. 14.

21. Erling Jorstad, *The New Christian Right: 1881-1988.* Studies in American Religion, vol. 25 (Lewiston/Queenstown: Edwin Mellen Press, 1987), p. 230.

22. *Minneapolis Star and Tribune,* July 31, 1984, p. 13A.

23. Quoted in Jorstad, p. 138.

24. Jerry Falwell, *Listen, America!* (New York: Bantam Books, 1980), Prologue.

25. Letter from Robert Grant's "Christian Voice," 1986.

26. NEA Human and Civil Rights "Bulletin," September 1984, p. 7, quoted in Jorstad, p. 192.

27. "Feminists and religious thinkers discuss 'threat' from the right," Religious News Service, January 14, 1986, p. 4.

Chapter 6

War Against the Constitution

You might ask: What is so bad about the New Christian Right's attempt to put in office people who would fight against abortion, the proliferation of pornography, drug abuse, and the rampant sexual promiscuity that is destroying Americans morally, spiritually, and now physically?

Should we be opposed to the philosophy that asserts, "The man who does not know God as his Father, and Jesus Christ as the only begotten Son of the Infinite God, cannot rule wisely"?

We better not, because that quote was not from Jimmy Swaggart, Jerry Falwell, or Pat Robertson.

Try—Ellen White![1]

Pollster George Gallup has said that the United States faces a "moral and ethical crisis of the first dimension."[2] The New Christian Right, aware of this festering sore on the soul of our country, tries to apply biblical principles to heal it.

"I have seen the grim statistics on divorce, broken homes, juvenile delinquency, promiscuity, and drug addiction," says Jerry Falwell on the back of his book *Listen, America!* "I have witnessed firsthand the human wreckage and shattered lives that statistics can never reveal in their totality. I am convinced that we need a spiritual and moral revival in America if America is to survive the twentieth century."

Many Americans, even secularists, agree that America needs spiritual and moral renewal—and few citizens expect the Playboy Foundation, Gary Hart, or the Ku Klux Klan to initiate it.

What, then, is wrong with these things that the New Christian Right is advocating?

Nothing.

The New Christian Right does not threaten to make America speak like a dragon because they oppose pornography, abortion, drug use, or sexual immorality, nor because they want godly people in office. On the contrary, we can and should support them on these issues.

Some people, though, are bothered by the New Christian Right's use (or misuse) of Scripture. They use the Bible to back the South African government, increased defense spending, aid to the Contras, support for Taiwan, and Star Wars, among other issues, such as gun-control laws.

Yet the New Christian Right is not the first, nor will it be the last, to use the Bible to sanction a potpourri of political idealogies. Compared, though, to the Church of England in the sixteenth and seventeenth centuries—when it used the Bible to justify imprisonment, banishment, torture, and death of thousands of dissenters—the New Christian Right's exegetical ability to get support for Taiwan out of the Bible is not the stuff dragons are made of.

And neither are they the first, nor the last, to believe God is on their side. "You have not set yourself against the hick fundamentalists," Jimmy Swaggart once said to an opponent. "You have set yourself against God."[3]

The New Christian Right does not pose the threat shown in Revelation 13 because it uses the Bible, however creatively, to advocate support for Star Wars, Taiwan, or even South Africa—or even because they believe God sanctions these positions. Instead, the threat comes from their unabashed hostility to the wall of separation of church and state—the principle that has kept America in the lamblike phase of the beast of Revelation 13:11!

" 'Separation of church and state' is a false issue," said New Right leader and former congressman and Arizona state Senator John B. Conlan. "It is a slogan created by the secular humanists which sounds legal, but in fact is a sham. It does not appear anywhere in the constitution, and it is not a concept that our Founding Fathers believed. . . . 'Separation of church and state' . . . is simply a line of propaganda created by modern humanists to intimidate Christians and make us believe we are second-class citizens."[4]

"I believe that this notion of the separation of church and state," said W. A. Criswell, a leading Baptist minister and the final speaker at the 1984 Republican Convention in Dallas, "was the figment of some infidel's imagination."[5]

To many in the New Christian Right, the wall of separation of church and state is "hostile" to religious freedom, particularly Christian freedom, and is condemned as part of a "secular humanist conspiracy" to place America in the hands of "atheists and communists." It is damned as a "misleading metaphor," "a pile of stones here and there," and a "totalitarian concept." Pat Robertson has even linked the phrase "separation of church and state" to the Russian constitution, not ours.

In 1947, Supreme Court Justice Wiley Rutledge wrote that "we have staked the very existence of our country on the faith that complete separation between state and religion is best for the state and best for religion."[6]

In the 1830s, French philosopher and historian Alexis de Tocqueville, visiting America, wrote that Americans "all attributed the peaceful dominion of religion in their country mainly to separation of church and state. I do not hesitate to confirm that during my stay in America I did not meet a single individual, of the clergy or the laity, who was not of the same opinion."[7]

He'd meet a few today. A recent poll showed that one quarter of all Americans are *against* the concept of the separation of church and state![8] And we're not just talking about the ordinary man on the street. Some informed people hold the same views: "The 'wall of separation between church and state' is a metaphor based on bad history, a metaphor which has proved useless as a guide to judging," said United States Supreme Court *Chief* Justice William Rehnquist. "It should be frankly and explicitly abandoned."[9]

Lutheran historian Erling Jorstad, writing about the unexpected rise of the New Christian Right in American politics, says that "such rapid and carefully orchestrated involvement suggests that the American citizenry may be in the midst of a major reassessment of the traditional blend of religion and politics."[10]

Warning about the New Christian Right, Americans United president Bob Maddox said that "they have launched the most dangerous attack on the United States Constitution I have ever seen—perhaps the worst in the nation's history."[11]

The church-state struggle now raging in America is not over minor legal technicalities. It's more a battle for theologians and philosophers than lawyers. The issues involve a radical change in the philosophy regarding government role in religion, a change which—if in the direction that the New Christian Right advocates—could make this nation speak as a dragon.

"Today, in America," writes historian Franklin Littell, "religious liberty is in more serious jeopardy than it has been for many years. Let a single fact serve as a sign of the deteriorating situation in the U.S.A.: there are today, according to watchdog offices, between 4,000 and 6,000 cases before the courts involving religious liberty—far more than during the entire history of the republic from 1791 to 1980."[12]

Many of these cases involve the "establishment clause" of the First Amendment. Though for years the courts have consistently (with a few exceptions) refused to allow the state to promote, aid, or push any religious belief—with the idea that separation was best, not only for the state, but for religion itself—a new thrust, coming even from the most powerful levels of government, claims that this position is not only a wrong interpretation of the Constitution and American history, but that it is actually hostile to religious freedom. They claim that the First Amendment allows the government to give "nondiscriminatory" aid to religion, that it allows the government to advance, promote, even pay for religion, just as long as government does not attempt to establish one "national religion."

Dissenting in a 1985 school prayer case, Chief Justice Rehnquist said that the framers of the Constitution intended only "to prohibit the designation of any church as a national one [and] to stop the Federal Government from asserting a preference of one religious denomination or sect over others." He believes the Constitution does not prevent the federal government from promoting religion in general, or from preferring religion over irreligion.

Yet, as we studied earlier, the First Amendment—no matter how carefully read, analyzed, parsed, or exegeted— was framed to *deny* power to the government. If the Constitution itself never originally gave the government the right to deal with religion in the first place, the First Amendment then denies power that the government never had. Constitutional scholar Leonard Levy warns that to argue that "the establishment clause should be construed to permit nondiscriminatory aid to religion leads to the impossible conclusion that the First Amendment *added* to the powers of Congress even though it was framed to restrict

Congress. It is not only an impossible conclusion; it is ridiculous."[13]

Yet, today, a whole bevy of scholars, government leaders, and clergymen accept a new interpretation of the Constitution, one that allows the government to promote religious beliefs. Because they interpret the establishment clause as forbidding only the establishment of one "national" religion, not aid to religion in general, and because the Constitution itself does not forbid general aid to general religion, Madison's fears about an abuse of the Constitution are coming true. "Madison was fearful," wrote author John Swomley, "that a bill of rights might be construed by future advocates of governmental power as implying that the government had implied powers that were not specifically denied to it. Madison's fears have been realized."[14]

The battle now rages. One of the hottest issues is that of government-sponsored prayer in school, or government-sponsored time for prayer in school. The controversy began with *Engle v. Vitale* in 1962, when the Supreme Court banned state-led prayer in public schools. It surfaced again in *Wallace v. Jaffree* in 1985, when the Supreme Court struck down an Alabama law allowing one minute for "meditation or voluntary prayer."

These decisions have been attacked as an infringement upon free exercise of religion. Tim LaHaye called the *Jaffree* decision "an act of war against this nation's religious heritage." Jerry Falwell declared: "Surely the United States of America, which presents itself a nation under God, can only be viewed as hypocritical when it refused to tell its children that they may pray to God."[15]

Yet no law forbids children to pray in school. They can pray all they want, when they want, and if they don't disturb the class—they can even pray out loud. The issue is not whether they are allowed to pray. The issue is whether the government should be in the business of promoting prayer, which is nothing but a religious exercise. To advocate prayer, or even a time for prayer, is not neutrality toward religion but an establishment of it, which the First Amendment forbids.

Other decisions attacked as anti-God are *Abingdon School District v. Schempp* and *Murray v. Curlett* (1963), which forbade Bible readings in school as part of a religious exercise. These decisions were attacked then, and still are today, with the usual rhetoric about God being kicked out of schools and about how Voltaire and Balzac can be read in school, but not the Holy Bible. Yet the Bible can be read in the public school system. The decisions outlawed only state-sponsored devotional readings of the Bible in public schools, not the Bible itself. The High Court specifically said that the Bible could be "part of a secular program of education." The decisions did not forbid private devotional readings by students, even on school grounds. It simply stopped the schools themselves from using the Bible in religious services. Far from being hostile to religious freedom, the decisions protect it.

Imagine, for instance, a Jewish child's humiliation if the teacher were to read the verse in Revelation about the "synagogue of Satan." How would a Catholic child feel about the reading of 2 Thessalonians 2:3 with its reference to the "man of sin," historically identified as the pope by Protestants? What about the atheist child who must listen to the verse in the Psalms that reads: "The fool hath said in his heart, There is no God"? These children, forced by law to attend school, must listen to this religious indoctrination or face the humiliation of leaving the classroom. In the 1800s, when the Bible was read in public schools, canon law forbade Catholics from reading or even possessing Protestant versions of the Bible, such as King James. Refusing to participate in worship services, Catholic children were punished, expelled, beaten. In Philadelphia, riots broke out, people were killed, and Catholic churches burned over the issue. *Abingdon* and *Murray,* by prohibiting the schools to intrude in religion, protect this nation from a repeat performance.

Other areas of contention deal with government money to religion. Though the court has upheld tax-exemption for churches (Madison opposed it), which keeps millions and millions of extra dollars each year in church coffers, dollars that need to be collected from other citizens—for some, that benefit is not enough. They want more. Though the Supreme Court has allowed the use of federal funds for transportation of children to parochial schools, the loan of textbooks to parochial schools, and federal grants for the construction of nonsectarian buildings on religious campuses, numerous churches are holding out the collection plate for Uncle Sam to drop in millions more. In most cases, the Supreme Court has said No to various attempts to get the government to pay for religious instruction. These decisions, too, have been attacked as part of a conspiracy against America's religious heritage.

Yet the First Amendment reads that the government shall not make any law "respecting an establishment of religion," and, as a Supreme Court justice once noted, the most effective way to establish any religion is to "finance it."

When the government funds a religious school, in effect a Protestant is paying for the promotion of Catholic or Jewish beliefs, or vice versa. How free is the Jew who pays taxes that promote Roman Catholicism, which teaches that the priest can turn a piece of bread into the body of God, blasphemy to a Jew? How free is the Catholic who pays taxes to support a Lutheran school, when Martin Luther called Pope Paul III "the scum of all the scoundrels in Rome"?

In America, we can't be forced to pay taxes even to our own religion, must less other ones.

These and other court decisions that have forbidden the

government to promote religion don't reflect hostility to faith in God. Instead, they simply say to the country, Pray, read your Bibles, build your schools—but don't ask the government to advance, promote, or pay for it! This principle, the basic foundation of church-state separation, has given Americans unprecedented religious freedom.

But what do these issues have to do with last-day events? What do a few prayers or Bible readings in school have to do with the issue concerning the mark of the beast? Do Supreme Court decisions regarding Bible reading or school prayer, even if reversed—as the New Christian Right wants—have any relevance to a national Sunday law?

They do. On the surface, the question seems to deal only with the establishment of religion, not the free exercise of it. After all, how could a law allowing devotional reading of the Bible in public schools lead to the enforcement of Sunday worship?

The real issue in all these cases *is* the free exercise of religion. As we saw earlier, the only way to have true religious freedom is to establish no religious belief by law. Those whose beliefs might conflict with the legally established norms would then face the threat of those laws.

The basic purpose of the establishment clause was to avoid an infringement upon free exercise by not allowing any one religious belief to become law. Once we get establishment, free exercise will be compromised. "Put differently," said Richard John Neuhaus, "the free exercise of religion requires the nonestablishment of religion."[16] What the New Christian Right advocates *is* an establishment of religion, the first step toward the persecution of those who "keep the commandments of God."

The only way for Sunday to be enforced, not a civil Sunday, but a religious Sunday—which is what it will eventually become—will be if the establishment clause is either abolished, ignored, or reinterpreted. As long as the First Amendment retains its original meaning, which restricts the government from legislating religious dogma, America will not speak as a dragon. The New Christian Right and its allies want to remove that barrier. They believe the government should assume the prerogatives of establishing religion, either state-sponsored prayer in school or tax money to support religious schools. Once such a precedent is set, what would stop it from establishing Sunday worship by law too? Remove the establishment clause and America will be in a much easier position to "wage war against the church and the law of God."— Ellen G. White, *Signs of the Times,* November 1, 1899.

Already such forces are at work. The New Christian Right claims that we need prayer back in school for the good of the nation. "Voluntary Prayer in Public Schools. America's Last Chance" reads one of Falwell's media hypes. Teenage pregnancy, drug use, suicide, vandalism, and alcoholism are all linked to the fact that the government does not sponsor prayer in school.

The issues don't stop with children in school. "Modern man is, it seems, faced by the final challenge of history," wrote Ernest Lee Tuveson in *Redeemer Nation: The Idea of America's Millennial Role.* What is that role? To "create the millennium, or go down into the lake of fire."[17]

This theme, echoing for years, claims that either we get our act together as one nation under God, or we perish. Either we obey God, or we face His wrath. In *Listen, America!* Falwell quotes former chaplain of the Senate Peter Marshall, who said: "Today, we are living in a time when enough individuals, choosing to go to hell, will pull the nation down to hell with them. The choices you make in moral and religious questions determine the way America will go. The choice before us is plain, Christ or chaos, conviction or compromise, discipline or disintegration. I am rather tired of hearing about our rights and privileges as American citizens. The time has come, it now is, when we ought to hear about the duties and responsibilities of our citizenship. America's future depends upon her accepting and demonstrating God's government."[18]

God's government, of course, involves God's law—the Ten Commandments. "George Gallup said his findings indicate that a whopping 84 percent today in America believe that the Ten Commandments are valid, so we began putting together that Moral Majority," said Jerry Falwell.[19] According to Falwell, the Founding Fathers' goal "was to govern the United States of America under God's laws," which, he said, "are directly based on the Ten Commandments. Most of the Ten Commandments are still written into the statute laws in the various states."[20]

Almost everyone in the New Christian Right believes that the Ten Commandments are valid and should be the basic law of the land. Naturally, they were upset at the 1980 Supreme Court decision (*Stone v. Graham*) that banned the posting of the Ten Commandments in public-school classrooms. Said Jimmy Swaggart in a sermon of February 10, 1985: "The greatest breeding ground in this nation for alcohol and illicit sex . . . is the public-school system. It's because we have ignored God, ripped the Ten Commandments from our walls, and no longer regard our heavenly Father in our schools."

Included in the Ten Commandments, of course, is the fourth, which all the New Christian Right leaders believe should be kept on Sunday, in honor of the resurrection of Jesus. Jerry Falwell has publicly stated that he believes the Sabbath is Sunday, not Saturday—and Pat Robertson wrote that "the reason Christians worship on Sunday instead of Saturday is that Sunday is the day of the Resurrection. Jesus rose from the grave on Sunday, and the Christian church celebrates that day."[21]

Look at the factors. We have a powerful political group, one that came out of nowhere, to hold, as quoted earlier, "the most visible and assertive position in American politics." Blatantly hostile to the idea that the government should not establish religious values by law, the New Christian Right have openly prodded the government to enact the laws that reflect their religious values. Values based, they claim, on the Ten Commandments. They all see Sunday worship as one of those commandments.

One doesn't need a prophet to see where this situation could lead. Yet a prophet helps, and Ellen White wrote that the Catholics and Protestants in this nation will unite in persuading the government to establish Sunday as the national day of worship. "It will be declared that men are offending God by the violation of the Sunday sabbath; that this sin has brought calamities which will not cease until Sunday observance shall be strictly enforced."—*The Great Controversy,* page 590.

Clamors about the dangers of Sunday desecration are as old as America itself. Yet it has never been enforced as a religious day because the First Amendment restriction against establishing a religion has forbidden it. Yet should the current New Right sentiments regarding religious freedom prevail—that the government has the right to enforce religious laws—an enforced Sunday would be the inevitable result of a government that holds the Ten Commandments as the basic law of the land.

Today's argument that the official establishment of religious beliefs is in the public welfare will be used in the critical days ahead. State-sponsored prayer in schools, the Ten Commandments on the classroom wall, or tax money to go to churches all have a certain allure to Christian sentiment. If the claim is accepted that in order to save American youth, America needs to legislate a minute of silence for prayer, how easily, then, will proponents be able to bring in a Sunday law in order to save the entire nation, even the world, from destruction.

"It will be urged," Ellen White wrote, "that the few who stand in opposition to an institution of the church [i.e. Sunday] and a law of the state ought not to be tolerated; that it is better for them to suffer than for whole nations to be thrown into confusion and lawlessness."—*The Great Controversy,* page 615.

For decades both Catholics and Protestants, even when they killed each other in the streets, agreed on the need to keep Sunday holy. Though they have disagreed on numerous theological points, Sunday keeping has not been one of them. If anything, it has helped unite them into the powerful political coalitions of the past decade. For example, a delegation of conservative southern Protestants from the Lord's Day Alliance, "the only national organization whose sole purpose is the maintenance and cultivation of the first day of the week as a time for rest," (founded in 1888) went to Rome and on October 15, 1986, presented Pope John Paul II with a Plaque of Appreciation, which read: "The Lord's Day Alliance of the United States expresses appreciation to His Holiness Pope John Paul, II, for his outstanding service in preserving The Lord's Day throughout the world."[22]

Right now, Sunday legislation doesn't claim top billing in the New Christian Right's agenda for a moral revamping of America. That is presently reserved for Star Wars, AIDS, abortion, state-sponsored prayer in school, and aid to the Contras. Every now and then someone will refer to Sunday keeping. Usually it is mentioned only when some Adventist asks about it, to which the typical reply is that Sunday is the Sabbath day and perhaps it should be legislated.

In celebration of its 1888 centennial, the Lord's Day Alliance published a book called *The Lord's Day,* a compilation of thirty sermons, speeches, and articles presented over the years about Sunday worship. The theme of Sunday legislation was woven through the book like a fine and consistent thread.

One author said that he had " 'blue laws' embedded into [his] veins."[23] Wrote another: "We can seek to have laws that will grant the opportunity of a day of rest and worship for those who choose to use it."[24] "One can easily paint a true picture of the benefits the people of any nation would gain," wrote Harold Linsell, "if they obeyed God's natural law of one day of rest in seven. This would involve closing down all businesses, including gasoline stations and restaurants every Lord's Day."[25]

Lamenting the continual desecration of the Lord's Day, Galbraith Hall Todd wrote that the "laws of at least forty-seven of our states once had statutes which would constitute barriers to protect the people from those who would rob them of the Lord's Day." He then quoted a source, which said: "The Lord's Day (the Christian Sabbath) is placed in our hands by the authority of the apostles of Christ, under the undiminished sanction of the eternal law of God."[26]

"Truly," wrote Aaron Nekel, "Sunday is the core of our civilization."[27]

Though the Lord's Day Alliance claims that they do not now seek legislation to keep the day holy, a recent promotional brochure suggests otherwise. "We suggest that letters be written to editors, legislators, mayors, governors, congressmen, and the President of the United States and that we speak to our representatives in government about using their influence for passing Sabbath laws that are constitutional."

Constitutional Sabbath laws are those that stress Sunday, not as a day of worship, but as a day of rest for the family. In the early sixties, the United States Supreme Court held that most Sunday laws were "of a secular rather than religious character," and therefore constitutional. In 1985, the Canadian Supreme Court, for example, struck down Canada's national Sunday law, the Lord's Day Act, as unconstitutional, declaring that it "creates a climate hostile to and gives the appearance of discrimination against" those who don't concur with Sunday observance. Yet a year later, another Sunday-closing-law bill, this time without the religious title (it was called the Ontario Retail Business Holiday's Act) was upheld, even though the court admitted the bill infringed upon the rights of those who didn't keep Sunday.

Perhaps America's Sunday legislation will initially come, like Ontario's, dressed in the sheepskin of secular garb. One way or another, it will come—and if consistent with its stated aims, the New Christian Right would certainly work to bring out the wolf beneath it.

---

1. Letter 187, 1903.

2. Religious News Service, "Gallup says U.S. facing 'moral crisis of first dimension,'" April 22, 1987, p. 9.

3. Quoted in Erling Jorstad, *The New Christian Right* (Lewiston/Queenstown: Edwin Mellen Press, 1987), p. 167.

4. Quoted in Vern McLellan, *Christians in the Political Arena* (Charlotte, N.C.: Associated Press, 1986), p. 111.

5. Jim Buie, "Praise the Lord and Pass the Ammunition," *Church and State,* October 1984, p. 302.

6. Quoted in William Lee Miller, *The First Liberty* (New York: Alfred A. Knopf, 1986), p. 4.

7. Alexis de Tocqueville, *Democracy in America,* Phillips Bradley, ed. (New York: Alfred A. Knopf, 1963), vol. 1, p. 308.

8. Lowell Weicker, "Back to the Future," *Church and State,* March 1986, p. 11.

9. Quoted in Ed Doerr, "Americans for Religious Liberty," July 1987.

10. Jorstad, p. 230.

11. Quoted from a letter in 1986 by Dr. Robert L. Maddox.

12. Franklin Littell, "Religious Liberty in the U.S.A.," in *Religious Liberty and Human Rights,* Leonard Swindler, ed. (New York: Hippocrene Books), p. 17.

13. Leonard Levy, *The Establishment Clause* (New York: Mac-Millian Publishing Company, 1986), p. 116.

14. John Swomley, *Religious Liberty and the Secular State* (Buffalo, N.Y.: Prometheus Books, 1987), p. 23.

15. *Our Sunday Visitor*, June 23, 1985, p. 17. Quoted in Jorstad, p. 53.

16. Richard John Neuhaus, "Free exercise of religion—not establishment of religion—is the issue." Quoted in *NFD Journal*, August 1987, p. 3.

17. Ernest Lee Tuveson, *Redeemer Nation: The Idea of America's Millennial Role* (Chicago: University of Chicago Press, 1968), p. 231.

18. Quoted in Jerry Falwell, *Listen, America!* (New York: Bantam Books, 1980), p. 20.

19. Quoted in Norman Gulley, *Is the Majority Moral?* (Washington, D.C.: Review and Herald Publishing Assn., 1981), p. 21.

20. Falwell, p. 45.

21. Pat Robertson *Pat Robertson Answers* (New York: Thomas Nelson Publishers, 1984), p. 145.

22. "Lord's Day Alliance officials have audience with Pope John Paul II and others in Europe," *Sunday: The Magazine of the Lord's Day Alliance of the United States*, October/December 1986, pp. 8, 9.

23. James P. Wesberry, ed., *The Lord's Day* (Nashville, Tenn.: Broadman Press, 1986), p. 123.

24. *Ibid.*, p. 101.

25. *Ibid.*, p. 144.

26. *Ibid.*, p. 178.

27. *Ibid.*, p. 206.

Chapter 7

In Pursuit of the Millennium

In 1986, Pat Robertson challenged Jack Kemp and George Bush for delegates to the Michigan Republican party convention. After Robertson did well, he sent a letter to supporters stating: "THE CHRISTIANS HAVE WON! . . . What a breakthrough for the kingdom."[1]

Robertson's letter epitomizes the irony about the New Christian Right thrust into politics, an irony that—while inconsistent with their understanding of last-day events—fits the Adventist-held scenario perfectly.

Most New Christian Right Protestants are premillennialists. Like Adventists, they believe that Jesus will return prior to the establishment of the millennium. Before the second coming of Jesus, they believe that the world will face a terrible time of trouble, a surge of war, crime, and apostasy unlike anything ever previously experienced. They call that period the "great tribulation." Some, like Falwell, believe that Christians will be raptured from the planet just before the tribulation; others, like Robertson, believe Christians will live through it. Either way, their theology of last-day events, which includes an increase in lawlessness, violence, and war somehow doesn't seem to jive with their present attempt to control the most powerful nation in the world and legislate it back to the law of God.

Historian Erling Jorstad wrote that the premillennialism

of the New Christian Right seems "ill-suited for democratic politics, asserting that only a handful of believers would be saved, and that all humankind's strivings on earth would soon be destroyed."[2]

Why is Falwell trying to turn America back to God when he believes that at any time soon all faithful Christians will be taken off the earth, which will then plunge into unprecedented violence? Why bother to put only Christians in office, when they could all be suddenly raptured off the planet? Why does he constantly warn about God's wrath being poured on America when he knows that, according to the Bible, God's wrath will eventually be poured out on the whole world? Legislating America to biblical morality and righteousness seems to fly in the face of Bible predictions that evil will increase in the last days. Of course, Christians are to tarry until Jesus comes, and they should stand up against evil—but this is different from taking political control of the most powerful nation in the world.

Two premillennialist professors from Falwell's Liberty Baptist College write about the world America can create: "Imagine the world freed from the threat of domination by the 'evil empire' Soviet Russia and nations with similar goals.

"America and other nations could beat their swords into plowshares. . . .

"All the treasure and genius now harnessed for war could be marshaled for good. . . .

"No countries would face external obstacles to democracy and human rights. . . .

"Liberty and democracy would reign from pole to pole."[3]

Though fine in and of themselves, these utopian visions blatantly contradict everything their premillennialism teaches about conditions on the earth prior to the second coming. "Then shall be great tribulation," Jesus Himself said about those days (Matthew 24:21), "such as was not since the beginning of the world to this time, no, nor ever shall be."

What about Pat Robertson? He has written that Christians will go "through a time of tribulation until Jesus comes back." He believes that "there has always been a struggle between the people of God and those who serve Satan. Throughout history there have been successive martyrdoms of Christians, and it is the height of arrogance to assume that only twentieth-century Christians in the United States of America will be spared any kind of persecution. . . . There will be people during the Tribulation who love Jesus, and will give their lives for Him."[4]

Why, then, the bid for the presidency in order to bring Christian values back to America? He believes that in the period prior to the coming of Jesus, which is now, "those who refuse to accept Christ will grow worse and worse in their wickedness" and that "it will become increasingly difficult for the church and the world to coexist."[5] He believes the Bible teaches that true Christians in the last days will be persecuted, hated, suffering the wrath of the antichrist power, who does not allow them to buy or sell, and who eventually seeks to kill them. Somehow, that scenario doesn't fit in with the New Christian Right's thrust to control America by placing "Bible-believing Christians" into government positions.

"The tide is turning in our direction," says Tim LaHaye. "We're going to do it again and again and again, until we flood the country. . . . If every Bible-believing church in America would trust God to use them to raise up one person to run for public office in the next ten years, do you realize that we would have more Christians in office than there are offices to hold?"[6]

Other Christians have seen this inconsistency. Charismatic preacher David Wilkerson blasted the New Christian Right: "It sounds so pious, so spiritual and vital. Like Israel, many of God's people are crying for an Imperial pulpit—with a spiritual leader who will root out the entrenched powers of evil and legislate a new moral system. The pointed, accusing finger of thundering prophets and weeping watchmen is to be replaced by the refined pen of Christian congressmen enacting moral laws." This politicized church, Wilkerson said, "is not going to be the vehicle of Christ's dominion on earth, but rather the object of His wrath and abhorrence.

"You can be sure God has a people for Himself in these final days," Wilkerson continues, "but they are a despised, holy and separated remnant."[7]

Texas evangelist Stan McGehee warned about the New Right's venture into politics and its inconsistency with their understanding of last-day events: "Today, a popular theory among certain evangelicals is that Christians are to take over the world and present it to Christ when He returns. This view is in direct opposition to Biblical doctrine. Throughout the book of Revelation we see true Christians suffering persecution, not taking over the world! Likewise, Paul tells us that it is Christ's rule that will put down rebellion and ungodliness (1 Corinthians 15:24, 25). Alarmingly enough, the Bible speaks of man's established, religious-political rule as that of the antichrist!"[8]

Stan McGehee's last sentence was closer to the truth than he probably realized, and while the New Right's political ventures might be inconsistent with their eschatology—it fits the Adventists' perfectly! For over a hundred years we have been warning about the time when both Catholics and Protestants would join politically to unite church and state. The result, we know, will be the antichrist's reign of persecution.

What makes our understanding of last-day events even more dramatic is that Ellen White wrote of these events in *The Great Controversy* about a hundred years ago, at a time when the world was so different it might have been another planet. The book was published in 1888 (there's that year again), when anti-Catholicism, though not as bad as it had been, was nevertheless rampant. Indeed, many of her warnings against the papacy typified the Protestant sentiments of the time. In 1887, while she was writing it, the American Patriotic Association, a large anti-Catholic political party, was founded as a great wave of anti-Catholicism resurged (it had subsided during the Civil War). Yet, during this massive anti-Catholicism, she wrote that "the Protestants of the United States . . . will reach over the abyss to clasp hands with the Roman power; and . . . this country will follow in the steps of Rome in trampling on the rights of conscience."—*The Great Controversy,* page 588.

Such a prediction back then seemed about as plausible as if someone today predicted that the Ayatollah Khomeini would be the next president of the United States. Yet today the emergence of Protestant fundamentalists into the political arena fulfills that prophecy perfectly, especially because in some areas, such as church-state affairs, they are working with Roman Catholics—just as Ellen White predicted!

"The Roman Catholic bishops are also at work politically to end separation of church and state," warns author John Swomley. "They are working in an informal alliance with fundamentalist Protestants not only on the abortion issue, but to get government support of private church schools."[9]

"This is the first time in American history that there has been an all-out attack led by the Roman Catholic bishops, their fundamentalist Protestant counterparts, and the administration on separation of church and state. It remains to be seen whether the American principle of church-state separation will survive such a concerted effort. . . . The major Protestant denominations have been effectively silenced by ecumenism, falsely based on fear of offending the Catholic hierarchy."[10]

"All of us do want the nation's laws and policies to reflect the values, beliefs, and principles of America's Christian majority," wrote Gary Potter (*New York Times,* October 15, 1980), head of Catholics for Christian Political Action, a New Christian Right organization working for the same goals as Falwell and other Protestants. He added: "Why should not a nation's laws reflect the values, beliefs, and principles of the majority of the people? Those of such nations as Ireland and Israel do! Ours used to. They should again."

Of course, as Catholics and Protestants unite on political issues no one expects Jerry Falwell to start shouting, "Hail Mary!" or Pat Robertson to start praying to St. Jude. They don't need to. "To promulate its legislative agenda," wrote Erling Jorstad, "the New Christian Right constructs the rationale for its policy on the foundations of explicit theological doctrine. Its leaders recognize that to attract the support of those standing outside its doctrinal tradition (such as Mormons, Roman Catholics, Orthodox), they must refrain from demanding uniform consent to their dogmas. . . . What the leaders tell their nonfundamentalist colleagues is that although people of faith may differ over doctrines or forms of expression, absolute truth expressed in absolute theological dogma does exist. . . . On that basis, fundamentalists can have fellowship theologically and politically outside their carefully defined ground."[11]

Ellen White wrote that the churches would unite on what *they have in common,* which today consists of similar political goals established from a basic common theology. "When the leading churches of the United States, uniting upon such points of doctrine as are held by them in common, shall influence the state to enforce their decrees [prayer and Bible devotion in school, or Sunday worship?] and to sustain their institutions [tax money to their schools?], then Protestant America will have formed an image of the Roman hierarchy."—*The Great Controversy,* page 445.

Ellen White identified the lamblike beast of Revelation

13:11 as the United States. According to Revelation 13:12, this lamblike beast will cause the "earth and them that dwell therein to worship the first beast, whose deadly wound was healed." Only after the rough forge of two world wars did America rise as the great world power it is today—yet in the previous century this lamblike beast was identified as America. It was not openly apparent back then that America would fulfill a global rule.

The New Christian Right's plans don't end with America. They have a global vision, a worldwide strategy. Tim LaHaye talks about America's "moral revival" (remember, this is the revival that can come only after legislation) and says that "we could export it all over the world." Jerry Combee and Cline Hall of Liberty Baptist ask: "Is it America's destiny to deliver the world from tyranny?" Apparently, they believe so, and this deliverance involves America as being the "liberator of mankind and the leader of revolutionary progress in the world" and being "the launching pad for the evangelization of the world before the Second Coming of Christ."[12] America, they believe, has been selected "to be instrumental in the future of the world," but it must return to values that made America great.

The New Christian Right's rise into politics does fit one aspect of its understanding of last-day events. Almost all believe that Jesus will establish His millennial kingdom on the earth. Pat Robertson's victory cry in Michigan about a "breakthrough for the kingdom" makes more sense when we understand what he might possibly mean by "the kingdom." In his book *Pat Robertson Answers,* he explains that the millennium "is a transition period, when Jesus Christ comes back to earth to show mankind what it would have been like if sin had never entered the world. It will be a time when Jesus Christ will reign as king, and the kingdom of God will be established on the earth."[13]

Robertson's "breakthrough" for the kingdom, added to the Combee and Hall's spiritual and political jingoism about America's role of evangelizing the world, make an interesting combination in light of Ellen White's warning: "Papists, Protestants, and worldlings will alike accept the form of godliness without the power [the weak Christianity discussed in chapter 5], and they will see in this union a grand movement for the *conversion of the world and the ushering in of the long-expected millennium.*"—*The Great Controversy,* pages 588, 589. Italics supplied.

Could the New Christian Right's thrust into politics be a subconscious attempt to help usher in the "long-expected millennium"? Even if that's not what they consciously have in mind now, by controlling the government they would be well positioned to deal with those whose noncooperation might "hinder" the initiation of the thousand years of peace and prosperity they are all expecting.

Of course, it wouldn't be the first time those professing to follow Jesus attempted to establish the kingdom on earth. During His early ministry, Jesus had an enthusiastic following who wanted to set Him upon an earthly throne, not just as a spiritual leader, but as a political king who would save His people from the Romans and usher in an era of peace. Jesus resisted because He knew that the kingdom of God was not established by government decree, court decisions, or legislative bodies. "The kingdom of God," He said (Luke 17:21), "is within you."

Some still want to usher in the kingdom by use of the sword. Others look to the ballot box. Either way, Jesus no more needs their help now than He did back then. Indeed, Daniel teaches that when the kingdom of God comes, it will be by a "stone . . . cut out without hands" (Daniel 2:34), a stone that crushes all earthly kingdoms—perhaps even a misdirected Christianized America—until all nations become "like chaff of the summer threshingfloors; and the wind carried them away, that no place was found for them" (Daniel 2:35). Doesn't exactly sound as if He needs Pat in the White House to help.

New Christian Right apologists try to paint Jesus as a political activist. Jesus cannot fit these claims. Indeed, so faithfully did He adhere to the separation of church and state that when a man asked, "Speak to my brother, that he divide the inheritance with me," Jesus refused. "Man," He responded, "who made me a judge or a divider over you?" Luke 12:13, 14. His mission was spiritual, not political, and He gave man spiritual, not political advice: "Take heed, and beware of covetousness: for a man's life consisteth not in the abundance of the things which he possesseth." Verse 15.

Perhaps the closest Jesus came to initiating a national reform was when He cleansed the temple of the sheep and cattle scalpers whose irreverent racket gave the place all the dignity of a flea market. But even here, when He shouted, "Take these things hence" (John 2:16), the shysters fled, not because they feared His political clout, but because He spoke with the authority of God. The battle then, as now, is spiritual, not political, and Jesus employed spiritual, not political pressure—the only kind that works the type of change He desires.

Conservative Christians of the New Christian Right should understand this principle better than most. Instead they have embarked on a course that could lead them to fulfill prophecy in a manner that they seem not to anticipate.

Though America is still in the lamblike phase of the beast of Revelation 13:11, we hover on the brink of its speaking like a dragon. The political philosophy of the New Christian Right, if translated into law, could do nothing but mold America into "the image of the beast."

You don't need to be an Adventist to see the threat developing. In a letter warning about the New Christian Right, United States Senator Lowell Weicker, Jr., warned that the New Right wants "to alter our nation's public policies as no other religious group had done before and to shape America into their own intolerant image."

Norman Redlich, dean of the New York University school of law, warned that the New Right's undermining of the First Amendment could lead to the "remaking of America in a Christian image."[14]

"It may be Ronald Reagan's most profound achievement as a politician though it is hardly noticed in the establishment world," wrote Anthony Lewis in the *New York Times* (October 8, 1984). "He has given political legitimacy, and power, to religious fundamentalists who want to make America into their image as a 'Christian nation.' "

Still at the comma? Not for long.

---

1. Fred Barnes, "Rarin' to Go," *The New Republic*, September 29, 1986, p. 15.

2. Erling Jorstad, *The New Christian Right* (Lewiston/Queenstown: Edwin Mellen Press, 1987), p. 107.

3. Jerry Combee and Cline Hall, p. 114.

4. Pat Robertson, *Pat Robertson Answers* (New York: Thomas Nelson Publishers, 1984), p. 156.

5. *Ibid.*, p. 30.

6. *Christianity Today*, December 13, 1985, p. 65.

7. David Wilkerson, "The Laodicean Lie!" printed in an undated newsletter by World Challenge, Inc., Lindale, Tex.

8. Stan McGehee, "Political Christianity," *The Living Word*, p. 5.

9. John Swomley, *Religious Liberty and the Secular State* (Buffalo, N.Y.: Prometheus Books, 1986), p. 124.

10. *Ibid.*, p. 139.

11. Jorstad, p. 13.

12. Combee and Hall, p. 117.

13. Robertson, p. 160.

14. "Feminists and religious thinkers discuss 'threat' from the right," Religious News Service, January 14, 1986, p. 4.

Chapter 8

Job—Message to the Remnant

What now? The New Christian Right and its plans for America, even for the world, certainly fits our understanding of last-day events. More than any other force in existence, it seems ready to make America into the image of the beast. But what will we face when it does?

For years, Adventists have speculated about the time of trouble. Books have been written, sermons preached, paintings painted to depict the turmoil and trouble ahead. Generations of Adventist children have hidden under the covers at night, scared to tears about the horrors their parents have said are coming. Even Ellen White warns that the time of trouble will be worse than what we expect.

But what will happen when it does come? What will be our experience when our freedoms are taken away and the United States, as Ellen White says, will "wage war against the church and the law of God"?

The answer is found, again, in the book of Job. In chapter 4 we saw how Job portrays the contrast between God's view of religious freedom and the devil's. But Job is filled with present truth for those who struggle through the time of trouble. Indeed, no biblical book gives a better picture of what "those who keep the commandments of God and have the faith of Jesus" will confront when the dangers depicted in the previous chapters come real!

Job lost everything. His family was killed, his property destroyed, his servants left him. His home, his oxen, his camels—all his means of support vanished.

When false Christianity is established in America, either by annulling, abolishing, or reinterpreting the Constitution, will not God's people lose everything too? "In the last great conflict of the controversy with Satan those who are loyal to God will see every earthly support cut off."—*The Desire of Ages,* page 121. Ellen White was given a dream about a company traveling on a road that became narrower and narrower until they abandoned everything—wagons, suitcases, horses, shoes, even their socks. Soon, all they had was a cord of faith, to which they clung for support. (See *Testimonies,* vol. 2, pages 594-597.) In the end, faith in God was all Job had, and it will be all that God's remnant will have also.

Job struggled alone. He had no one, nothing, to lean on. He had to stand for himself, just as will God's faithful when the world completely abandons God's principles of religious freedom and God's remnant are attacked by those wanting to usher in a millennium of peace. "In that time of trial, every soul must stand for himself before God. 'Though Noah, Daniel, and Job' were in the land, 'as I live, saith the Lord God, they shall deliver neither son nor daughter; they shall but deliver their own souls by their righteousness.' Ezekiel 14:20."—*The Great Controversy,* pages 622, 623.

Satan twice told God that if God removed the hedge around him, Job would "curse thee to thy face." Job 1:11; 2:5. What did Job's wife tell him to do? "Curse God, and die," she said. Verse 9. The exact thing that Satan wanted Job to do, he suggested through Job's wife! You can almost see Satan whispering in her ear. The one closest to Job, his wife, became a tool of the devil against him.

Jesus recognized this natural antagonism between righteousness and disobedience. "I am come to set a man at variance against his father, and the daughter against her mother, and the daughter in law against her mother in law," the Lord predicted. "And a man's foes shall be they of his own household." Matthew 10:35, 36.

In the context of the time of trouble, Ellen White wrote that "all will be required to render obedience to human edicts in violation of the divine law. Those who will be true to God and to duty will be menaced, denounced, and proscribed. They will be betrayed 'both by parents, and brethren, and kinsfolks, and friends.'"—*Testimonies,* vol. 9, page 231.

Notice the calamities that befell Job. "The fire of God" came down from heaven and burned up sheep and servants. Job 1:16. Bands of Chaldeans and Sabeans stole his oxen, camels, and killed other servants. Verses 14, 15, 17. Then a wind blew down his house and killed his children. Verse 19. He faced a natural disaster—the wind. Supernatural disaster—"the fire of God." And manmade disaster—the Sabeans and Chaldeans attacking his property.

Job's friends accused him of causing these calamities!

"Think now," said Eliphaz, "who that was innocent ever perished? Or where were the upright cut off? As I have seen, those that plow iniquity and sow trouble reap the same." Job 4:7, 8, RSV.

"Know then that God exacts of you," said Zophar, "less than your guilt deserves." Job 11:6, RSV.

Throughout the speeches, Job was blamed for bringing the disasters: the supernatural judgment, the manmade strife, and the convulsion of nature—the exact things that God's people will be accused of causing! Already, the New Christian Right blames many of the ills and woes of the nation upon our sins, including desecration of the "Lord's Day."

"Those who honor the law of God have been accused of bringing judgments upon the world, and they will be regarded as the cause of the fearful convulsions of nature [great wind] and the strife and bloodshed among men [Sabean and Chaldean raids] that are filling the earth with woe."—*The Great Controversy,* page 614.

"Those who honor the Bible Sabbath will be denounced as enemies of law and order, as breaking down the moral restraints of society, causing anarchy and corruption, and calling down the judgments of God ["the fire of God"] upon the earth."—*The Great Controversy,* page 592.

Job's friends were not infidels or heathen, but religious men who, in some areas, had a knowledge of God. At one time they might have bowed their heads together in the dust as they prayed and worshiped with Job. Yet now, instead of coming to his aid, they misrepresented and accused him.

"As the storm approaches, a large class who have professed faith in the third angel's message, but have not been sanctified through obedience to the truth, abandon their position and join the ranks of the opposition. . . . They become the most bitter enemies of their former brethren . . . [and] are the most efficient agents of Satan to *misrepresent and accuse them.*"—*The Great Controversy,* page 608. Italics supplied.

Job's accusers threw all sorts of ammunition against him in order to make him admit his errors and that his understanding of God was incorrect.

"Amid thoughts from visions of night," said Eliphaz the Temanite, "when deep sleep falls on men, dread came upon me, and trembling, which made all my bones shake. A spirit glided past my face; the hair of my flesh stood up. It stood still, but I could not discern its appearance. A form was before my eyes; there was silence, then I heard a voice." Job 4:13-16, RSV.

Eliphaz had some type of occult experience. A spirit told him things that he recounted in his polemic against Job. He used spiritualism against Job. Will we not face the same thing? Indeed, the New Christian Right's belief in the immortality of the soul sets them up for this deception!

"The miracle-working power manifested through spiritualism will exert its influence against those who choose to obey God rather than man. Communications from the *spirits* will declare that God has sent them to convince the rejecters of Sunday of their error, affirming that the laws of the land should be obeyed as the laws of God."—*The Great Controversy,* pages 590, 591. Italics supplied.

Look what Bildad threw at Job: "Inquire, I pray you, of bygone ages, and consider what the fathers have found; for we are but of yesterday, and know nothing, for our days on earth are a shadow. Will they not teach you, and tell you, and utter words out of their understanding?" Job 8:8-10, RSV.

He tried scholarship, intelligence, to convince Job of his errors. He resorted to the wisdom of the fathers, to what the great men of old believed. Ellen White indicates that these were the arguments used in her time to convince people of Sunday. There is no question that they will be used again against God's people, just as they were against Job.

In the spirit's speech to Eliphaz, he said to him: "Can mortal man be righteous before God? Can a man be pure before his maker? Even in his servants he puts no trust, and his angels he charges with error; how much more those who dwell in houses of clay." Job 4:17-19, RSV.

Eliphaz said: "What is man, that he can be clean? Or he that is born of a woman, that he can be righteous? Behold, God puts no trust in his holy ones, and the heavens are not clean in his sight; how much less one who is abominable and corrupt, and a man who drinks iniquity like water!" Job 15:14-16, RSV. Later Bildad said: "How then can man be righteous before God? How can he who is born of women be clean? Behold, even the moon is not bright, and the stars are not clean in his sight; how much less man, who is a maggot, and the son of man, who is a worm?" Job 25:4-6, RSV.

They were telling Job that he couldn't be righteous, couldn't be holy before God. Even the angels are dirty, they said, so how much dirtier are you.

These dangerous words were intended to discourage Job. He knew that he had done nothing to deserve what was happening to him. If Job could be convinced that he was in error, that he deserved what befell him, then he might have given up in despair, even let go of his hold on God—the only thing that sustained him. In the end, he might have done what Satan wanted him to do.

Adventists now confront this same theology, one that asserts that we can't be holy or righteous, or that we can't overcome. What this doctrine really says is that we can't keep God's law.

Imagine standing in chains before a court because we insist that we want to keep the Ten Commandments, including the fourth, when—thanks to the political efforts of Protestants and Catholics in America—Sunday has been designated as the official day of rest. Yet, under severe questioning, we say, "Well, I don't believe that we can really keep God's law anyway. We really can't be holy before God." We are going to suffer and die for a law that can't be kept? The description of God's saints are those who "*keep* the commandments of God." Obviously, then, they can be kept and will be kept by the remnant. A theology which teaches that victory is impossible is nothing more than Satan's attempt to set us up for the mark of the beast, to turn us away from serving the true God, just as it was designed to turn away Job.

"Through defects in the character, Satan works to gain control of the whole mind, and he knows that if these defects are cherished, he will succeed. Therefore he is constantly seeking to deceive the followers of Christ with his fatal sophistry that it is impossible for them to overcome."—*The Great Controversy,* page 489.

This dangerous teaching was used against Job, and God's people face it too.

How did Job react to their accusations? What was his response? "Teach me, and I will be silent; make me understand how I have erred." Job 6:24, RSV. Job told them to show him where he was wrong. What will God's people say when they are challenged because of their position regarding the Sabbath? "Show us from the word of God our error."—*The Great Controversy,* page 607. Like Job, they, too, will challenge their opponents to prove where they are wrong.

Perhaps the most amazing aspect of the speeches was that not everything these men said to Job was wrong! On the contrary, much of what they said was correct. The words were filled with sublime and deep truth. They confronted Job with a mixture of truth and error.

Eliphaz at times sounds like Solomon. "Behold," he said, "happy is the man whom God reproves; therefore despise not the chastening of the Almighty. For he wounds, but he binds up; he smites, but his hands heal." Job 5:17, 18, RSV.

When Paul in 1 Corinthians 3:19, RSV, wrote, "For it is written, 'He catches the wise in their craftiness,'" he was quoting Job 5:13, the words of Eliphaz.

Elihu said, "Behold, God is mighty, and does not despise any; he is mighty in strength of understanding." Job 36:5, RSV. He also said, "Behold, God is great, and we know him not; the number of his years is unsearchable." Verse 26, RSV.

Said Zophar, "Can you find out the deep things of God? Can you find out the limit of the Almighty? It is higher than heaven—what can you do? Deeper than hell—what can you know?" Job 11:7, 8, RSV.

All through their speeches to Job, speeches which the Lord later said were wrong, these men spoke truth along with error. Much of what the New Christian Right advocates today is a mixture of truth and error too. We can agree with many of the positions they hold. Yet we have been warned that we will face a mixture of truth with falsehood. When, for example, Satan impersonates Christ in a false second coming, his "voice is soft and subdued, yet full of melody. In gentle, compassionate tones he presents some of the same gracious, heavenly truths which the Saviour uttered; . . . in his assumed character of Christ, he claims to have changed the Sabbath to Sunday, and commands all to hallow the day which he has blessed."—*The Great Controversy,* page 624.

Other parallels exist between Job's experience and what God's people will face. As Satan accused Job before the Lord, he also was allowed to try Job to the uttermost. God's latter-day people will confront the same test. "As Satan accuses the people of God on account of their sins, the Lord permits him to try them to the uttermost. Their confidence in God, their faith and firmness, will be severely tested. As they review the past, their hopes sink. . . . [Satan] hopes so to destroy their faith that they will yield to his temptations and turn from their allegiance to God."—*The Great Controversy,* pages 618, 619. Satan hoped to do the same to Job, to so discourage him that he would turn his allegiance away from God and, indeed, curse God to His face.

Job suffered; we will suffer. Job cried out to God for deliverance; God's people will "day and night . . . cry unto God for deliverance."—Page 630. The trials became worse for Job; they will become worse for us. Though Satan was allowed to torment, harass, and severely persecute Job, he was not allowed to kill him. Though, after probation closes, Satan will be allowed to torment, harass, and persecute God's people, he will not be allowed to kill them. Indeed, just as Job didn't die in this trial, God's remnant will not be allowed to die in their great time of trial, either. (See *Testimonies,* vol. 9, page 17; *The Great Controversy,* pages 633, 634.)

Another obvious parallel is that Job remained faithful. He

endured to the end, just as the Lord will have a people who endure to the end of time. "I saw what appeared to be a sea of glass mingled with fire, and those who had conquered the beast and its image and the number of its name, standing beside the sea of glass with harps of God in their hands." Revelation 15:2, RSV.

Yet why did Job remain faithful? Why didn't he "curse God and die," as the devil wanted him to, as many would have in similar circumstances? Job, obviously, had been prepared for this trial. And, as we will see, Job's preparation didn't come instantly. It didn't happen to Job overnight, just before the day of destruction. On the contrary, he had been preparing for years. How? By having formed a "Christian" character through obedience to God, the only way anyone will be able to stand in the time of trouble.

In chapter 31 of the book, Job mentions the things he had done over the years which showed that he had been forming a righteous character. In verse 1 he said that he did not lust after women. In verse 5 he said that he had not "walked with falsehood." Through the chapter he says that he was not covetous (verse 7), not an adulterer (verse 9), and had not mistreated his servants (verse 13). He had been kind to the poor, the widow, the fatherless (verses 16, 17). He did not make "gold [his] trust" (verse 24), nor did he rejoice because his wealth was great (verse 25). He avoided idolatry (verses 26, 27), nor did he rejoice in the ruin of his enemies (verse 29). He was hospitable (verse 32), had confessed his sins (verse 33), and was a good steward of his land (verse 38-40). In short, Job had lived a godly life, one that exemplified Christian virtues.

This godly life gave him the faith that enabled him to endure to the end, no matter the great trials. As Scripture records of Abraham: "By works was faith made perfect." James 2:22.

Job is no display of salvation by works. Job was a sinner; he knew that he needed a Redeemer. "I know," he cried, "that my redeemer liveth." Instead, by a life of humble obedience filled with good works, Job formed a special relationship with God that enabled him to stand in his time of trial.

Jesus taught this principle in Matthew 7:24-27, in the story of one who hears His commands and "doeth them." Jesus likened him to a "wise man," one who built his house upon a rock, "and the rain descended, and the floods came, and the winds blew, and beat upon that house; and it fell not." Why? Because it was founded on the rock. How was it founded on the rock? Because the man was obedient to the things he heard Jesus say, in contrast to the man who heard the commands but "doeth them not," whose house washed away in the flood.

Job, by obedience, had built his house on the Rock. So when the wind came, it was not taken away. Like Job, those who have the faith to stand in the time of trouble will have built on the Rock. Yet, like Job, the preparation must begin before the time of trouble. The time to prepare is now, before America speaks as a dragon; otherwise we will be enticed or frightened into submission by its false words.

"I saw that many were neglecting the preparation so needful and were looking to the time of 'refreshing' and the 'latter rain' to fit them to stand in the day of the Lord and to live in His sight. Oh, how many I saw in the time of trouble without a shelter! They had neglected the needful preparation; therefore they could not receive the refreshing that all must have to fit them to live in the sight of a holy God."—*Early Writings,* page 71.

What is this preparation? It is the same process Job spoke of. "Unless we are daily advancing in the exemplification of the *active Christian virtues,* we shall not recognize the manifestations of the Holy Spirit in the latter rain."—*Tes-*

timonies to Ministers, page 507. Italics supplied.

Three times the Bible says that Job was "perfect." Twice God says it Himself (Job 1:8; 2:3)! Other versions use the word *blameless* (RSV, NEB). In all his trial, "Job sinned not, nor charged God foolishly" (Job 1:22); and "in all this did not Job sin with his lips." Job 2:10.

Was Job a sinner? Of course. "The scripture hath concluded all under sin, that the promise by faith of Jesus Christ might be given to them that believe." Galatians 3:22. Job knew he was a sinner: "Thou writest bitter things against me, and makest me inherit the *iniquities of my youth.*" Job 13:26, RSV. Italics supplied. Job will not make it to heaven because of his own righteousness, which is "as filthy rags," but only because of the righteousness of Jesus in place of his, the righteousness that comes by faith.

Nevertheless, Job had formed a special character, one that enabled him to endure a terrible time of trouble—and not break God's law.

God's people will have the same experience, even though all the power of the church and state is set against them. God's people are described as those who "keep the commandments of God, and the faith of Jesus." Revelation 14:12. The text doesn't say those who keep "the commandment of God," but the commandments of God, *plural.* We have tended to look at that text as referring only to the Sabbath, but it refers to all the commandments of God, His entire law. God will have a people who keep all His commandments.

"Are we seeking His fullness, ever pressing toward the mark set before us—the perfection of His character? When the Lord's people reach this mark, they will be sealed in their foreheads. Filled with the spirit they will be complete in Christ, and the recording angel will declare, 'It is finished.' "

"I also saw that many do not realize what they must be in order to live in the sight of the Lord without a high priest in the sanctuary through the time of trouble. Those who receive the seal of the living God and are protected in the time of trouble must reflect the image of Jesus fully."—*Early Writings,* page 71.

The book of Job is a microcosm, one man's experience of what will happen to thousands when the whole world, under the leadership of America, makes war against God's law. Satan made accusations against the Lord. By remaining faithful, by not succumbing to temptation, Job proved Satan wrong.

This same situation will occur in the last days, though on a grander, more climactic scale. Just as with Job, God is going to use His people to prove wrong Satan's accusations against the divine government, law, and justice.

Ephesians 3:10 says that "through the church the manifold wisdom of God might now be made known to the principalities and powers in the heavenly places." RSV. Notice this text says that "through the church," the wisdom of God is going to be made known to powers in the universe. This text does not take away from the cross; instead, it simply shows that as far as the whole universe is concerned, all the questions were not answered there. God, apparently, intends to answer these questions through His church. In *The Acts of the Apostles,* page 9, Ellen White writes that "through the church will *eventually* be made manifest, even to 'the principalities and powers in heavenly places,' the final and full display of the love of God." Italics supplied.

Jesus said, "Herein is my Father glorified, that ye bear much fruit." John 15:8. God is glorified if we bear much fruit. What is the first angel's message? "Fear God and give *glory* to him." And how do we give Him glory? By bearing much fruit. Ellen White says it plainly: "The honor of God, the honor of Christ, is involved in the perfection of the character of His people."—*The Desire of Ages,* page 671.

Satan accused God before the "sons of God," other powers in the universe. "Doth Job fear God for naught?" (Job 1:9) he asked, insinuating that Job served God, not out of love, but because it was in Job's own selfish interest. Inherent in Satan's accusation was the charge that God's creatures didn't serve Him for the right reasons. If God was so good, His government and laws so fair, would His creatures be loyal no matter what? Satan said No, and God proved him wrong. The firm loyalty of Job brought glory to God.

So, too, will God's faithful remnant be privileged to stand for God. Like Job, they will be attacked by Satan. This time Satan uses apostate Protestants and Catholics who have merged church and state into a despotic system much like the one that ruled Europe for over a thousand years. Yet like Job, by staying faithful, the remnant will, in the "full and final display"—bring glory to God. If God could be glorified through Job's faithfulness, how much greater will be the testimony of this group?

Indeed, despite the tremendous economic, family, theological, and physical pressure brought upon God's remnant, despite having all the powers of the government and church arrayed against them, despite the devil's frantic attempt to turn them away from worshiping the Creator, despite pain, suffering, and delay—God's remnant, like Job, will stay obedient to His commandments and will, like Job, exclaim, even in the most adverse circumstances: "The Lord gave, and the Lord hath taken away; blessed be the name of the Lord!" Job 1:21.

The rise of the New Christian Right, together with its cooperation with Roman Catholics in an attempt to bring America back to the "Ten Commandments," more than any other event in recent years, should warn Adventists that the time of trouble is close, that the days the prophets wrote about are here. "The appearance of the New Christian Right," says

Erling Jorstad, "marks a significant new development in the history of the nation, and the history of the church."

Some might be tempted, however, to see Robertson's failed campaign as a sign of the New Right's demise. Hardly. Robertson will be back, and so will the New Right.

If anything, it might be to their advantage that Robertson lost. As far to the right as America has gone under Reagan, at this present rate it would take a hundred years before America would kill people for keeping Sabbath. But if a major economic catastrophe (which almost everyone expects) came—the situation could change instantly. Had a disaster struck under a Robertson presidency, people would blame him and the New Right. Instead, if a disaster happens under a Democrat, or even a moderate Republican, then the New Right will proclaim, "See, we told you so. Here is the judgment that we have warned about. This nation needs to get back to God. Let us lead you there." And the same Americans who now, under conditions of prosperity, basically told Robertson to go back to church, might then be ready to put him, or someone else like him, in power.

Of course, exactly how the end will happen, we don't know. What we do know is that we need to be prepared. We need an experience that many of us don't now have. We need the experience of Job.

We also need to warn others, even those in the New Right. For they, like us, are part of the prophets' dreams. Unless they are given an understanding of present truth—that dream could be their nightmare.